Critical Acclaim for
Writing a Woman's Life

"Astute and provocative. . . . Blends the sophistication of recent feminist theory with highly textured details from the lives of independent and ambitious women."

The New York Times Book Review

"A book of possibilities, for Heilbrun has turned her own, and other women's lives, into hopeful narratives, exemplary models for present and future generations to lean on."

The Boston Phoenix

"A clarion call to women to shed traditional female postures and forge new destinies. . . . Heilbrun celebrates women who do not make a man the center of their lives; adventurous, pioneering women in search of new story lines such as going it alone or living with a younger, less accomplished mate; women who wish to make an impact in the public domain; women who wish to live a 'quest plot,' like men. After all, observes Heilbrun, why should men have all the fun?"

New Woman

Critical Acclaim for *Writing a Woman's Life*

"Packed with insight and wisdom. . . . A sprightly, graceful and sometimes acerbic guide to what we might all aspire to become in life. . . . The best thing to do is to share it with someone else, because reading alone is not enough: Her book makes conversation, discussion, even argument absolute necessities."

Philadelphia Inquirer

"A delight to read, for Heilbrun never hesitates to talk straightforwardly about forbidden subjects. . . . Eloquent. . . . Inspiring. . . . Clever and memorable."

The Women's Review of Books

Critical Acclaim for *Writing a Woman's Life*

"Graceful, intelligent, and concise. . . . Covers a lot of territory, yet it does not sacrifice depth and breadth. Rather, it teases one's appetite while teaching one how to read the authenticity of a biography. It also teaches and confirms the importance of telling a true story, particularly when the words of the story are aligned with the entirety of an individual's life."

The Bloomsbury Review

"This brief collection of essays reads so effortlessly that it's all too easy to underestimate its profundity. . . . An inspiring selection for millions of near-mid-life women who will be searching for more positive images."

Booklist

"Lengths ahead of most attempts to formulate a feminist methodology for biography or criticism, Heilbrun's suggestions are compelling."

The Kirkus Reviews

Writing a Woman's Life

CAROLYN G. HEILBRUN

BALLANTINE BOOKS • NEW YORK

To Nancy K. Miller

Grateful acknowledgment is made to the following for permission to reprint previously published material:

Maxine Kumin: "The Archeology of a Marriage" (excerpt) from *The Retrieval System* by Maxine Kumin. Copyright © 1978 by Maxine Kumin. Reprinted by permission of Viking Penguin, Inc.

Denise Levertov: "Relearning the Alphabet" (excerpt) from *Poems 1968–1972*. Copyright © 1970 by Denise Levertov. Reprinted by permission of New Directions Publishing Corporation.

Audre Lorde: "Coal" (excerpt) from *Coal*, Poems, by Audre Lorde. Reprinted by permission of W. W. Norton & Company, Inc. Copyright © 1968, 1970, 1976 by Audre Lorde.

Adrienne Rich: "What Is Possible" (excerpt) from *Wild Patience Has Taken Me This Far, Poems, 1978–1981* by Adrienne Rich. Copyright © 1981 by Adrienne Rich. "Dear Adrienne: I'm calling you tonight" (excerpt) from *Your Native Land, Your Life*, Poems, by Adrienne Rich. Copyright © 1986 by Adrienne Rich. Both are reprinted by permission of W. W. Norton & Company, Inc.

Anne Sexton: "Housewife" from *All My Pretty Ones* by Anne Sexton. Copyright © 1962 by Anne Sexton. Reprinted by permission of Houghton Mifflin Company.

Library of Congress Catalog Card Number: 88-92863
ISBN: 0-345-36256-X

This edition published by arrangement with W. W. Norton & Company, Inc.

Cover design by James R. Harris

Cover painting *L'Edition de Luxe* (1910) by Lilian Westcott Hale courtesy of Museum of Fine Arts, Boston

Manufactured in the United States of America

First Ballantine Books Edition: September 1989

20   19   18   17   16   15   14   13   12

Acknowledgments

*M*Y MAJOR DEBT in this book is to the critics and writers whose work is listed in the "Works Cited" section, and to other feminist scholars I may have neglected to mention there. I want also to thank those graduate students who gallantly took part in the seminar I offered at Columbia in the fall of 1986 on women's biography and autobiography. They all taught me much, Susan Heath and Suvendi Perera most of all.

I am grateful to the National Endowment for the Humanities for an Independent Study and Research Fellowship that gave me time off from teaching to work on this book in 1983–84.

Susan Stanford Friedman and David Hadas have each proffered much needed wisdom. Tom F. Driver generously read through the entire manuscript and discussed my ideas with me; in the writing of this book, as ever, he sustained and corrected me. Nancy K. Miller, to whom this book is dedicated, was, throughout its writing, colleague, friend, enabler.

James Heilbrun, who lived with me and this book through many years, deserves special thanks for attentions to both beyond all conventional requirements or demands.

Introduction

*To justify an unorthodox life by writing
about it is to reinscribe the original violation, to
reviolate masculine turf.*

—NANCY K. MILLER

THERE ARE FOUR WAYS to write a woman's life: the woman herself may tell it, in what she chooses to call an autobiography; she may tell it in what she chooses to call fiction; a biographer, woman or man, may write the woman's life in what is called a biography; or the woman may write her own life in advance of living it, unconsciously, and without recognizing or naming the process. In this book, I shall discuss three of these four ways, omitting, for the most part, an analysis of the fictions in which many women have written their lives. For these stories in women's fiction, both the conventional and the subversive, have been examined in recent years with great brilliance and sophistication by a new generation of literary critics, and the work of these feminist critics has been so penetrating and persuasive that learning to read fictional representations of gender arrangements in our culture, whether of difference, oppression, or possibility, is an opportunity now available to anyone who will take the time to explore this vast and compelling body of criticism.

It has been otherwise with the lives of women. True, numberless biographies of women have appeared in recent years,

many of them making use of new feminist theory developed by
literary critics, psychologists, and historians. In 1984, I wrote
in an article in the *New York Times Book Review* that, since
1970, I had added seventy-three new biographies of women to
my library. That number has certainly doubled by now, and
yet there are countless biographies of women that I have not
acquired. In 1984, I rather arbitrarily identified 1970 as the
beginning of a new period in women's biography because *Zelda*
by Nancy Milford had been published that year. Its significance lay above all in the way it revealed F. Scott Fitzgerald's
assumption that he had a right to the life of his wife, Zelda, as
an artistic property. She went mad, confined to what Mark
Schorer has called her ultimate anonymity—to be storyless.
Anonymity, we have long believed, is the proper condition of
woman. Only in 1970 were we ready to read not that Zelda had
destroyed Fitzgerald, but Fitzgerald her: he had usurped her
narrative.

With equal arbitrariness, I would name 1973 as the turning
point for modern women's autobiography. The transformation
in question can be seen most clearly in the American poet,
novelist, and memoirist May Sarton. Her *Plant Dreaming Deep*,
an extraordinary and beautiful account of her adventure in
buying a house and living alone, published in 1968, eventually
dismayed her as she came to realize that none of the anger,
passionate struggle, or despair of her life was revealed in the
book. She had not intentionally concealed her pain: she had
written in the old genre of female autobiography, which tends
to find beauty even in pain and to transform rage into spiritual
acceptance. Later, reading her idealized life in the hopeful
eyes of those who saw her as exemplar, she realized that, in
ignoring her rage and pain, she had unintentionally been less
than honest. Changing times helped bring her to this realization. In her next book, *Journal of a Solitude*, she deliberately

set out to recount the pain of the years covered by *Plant Dreaming Deep*. Thus the publication of *Journal of a Solitude* in 1973 may be acknowledged as the watershed in women's autobiography.

I call it the watershed not because honest autobiographies had not been written before that day but because Sarton deliberately retold the record of her anger. And, above all other prohibitions, what has been forbidden to women is anger, together with the open admission of the desire for power and control over one's life (which inevitably means accepting some degree of power and control over other lives). Nor have those born earlier than Sarton honored the watershed, or deigned to notice it. No memoir has been more admired and loved in recent years than Eudora Welty's *One Writer's Beginnings*. Yet I think there exists a real danger for women in books like Welty's in the nostalgia and romanticizing in which the author, and we in reading them, indulge. Virginia Woolf remarked that "very few women yet have written truthful autobiographies."

Let us look at what Eudora Welty wrote about Jane Austen:

The felicity the novels have for us must partly lie in the confidence they take for granted between the author and her readers. We remember that the young Jane read her chapters aloud to her own lively, vocative family, upon whose shrewd intuition, practiced and eager estimation of conduct, and general rejoicing in character she relied almost as well as she could rely on her own. The novels still have the bloom of shared pleasure. The young author enjoyed from the first a warm confidence in an understanding reception. As all her work testifies, her time, her place, her location in society, are no more matters to be taken in question than the fact that she was a woman. She wrote from a perfectly solid and firm foundation, and her work is wholly affirmative. . . . Jane Austen was born knowing a great deal—for one thing, that the interesting situations of life can, and notably do, take place at home. In country parsonages the dangerous confrontations and the decisive skirmishes can very conveniently be arranged. [1969, 4-5]

The woman who wrote those words about Jane Austen in 1969 is the same woman who wrote *One Writer's Beginnings* in 1983. But the Jane Austen she describes is not the Jane Austen I or many others read today, nor do we believe in this account of the perfect family nourishing her happy talent. Similarly, I do not believe in the bittersweet quality of *One Writer's Beginnings,* nor do I suppose that the Eudora Welty there evoked could have written the stories and novels we have learned to celebrate. Welty, like Austen, has long been read for what she can offer of reassurance and the docile acceptance of what is given; she has been read as the avatar of a simpler world, with simpler values broadly accepted. In this both Austen and Welty have, of course, been betrayed. But only Welty, living in our own time, has camouflaged herself. Like Willa Cather, like T. S. Eliot's widow, she wishes to keep meddling hands off the life. To her, this is the only proper behavior for the Mississippi lady she so proudly is.

As her interviewer noted in the *Paris Review,* Welty is "extremely private and won't answer anything personal about herself or about friends" (273). Michael Kreyling reported that Welty prizes loyalty and gratitude and disapproves of critics who approach writers with "insufficient *tolerance* and *sympathy*" (414–15). There can be no question that to have written a truthful autobiography would have defied every one of her instincts for loyalty and privacy.

But why should I criticize Eudora Welty for having written the only autobiography possible to her? From what I know and have heard, she is the kindest, gentlest person imaginable. What then do I want from her? Would life not be preferable if we were all like Eudora Welty?

It would. Yet, since we are not, her genius as a writer of

stories rescues her and us from her nostalgia. But it is that nostalgia, rendered with all the charm and grace of which she is capable, that has produced this autobiography, that same nostalgia that has for so many years imprisoned women without her genius or her rewards. Nostalgia, particularly for child-hood, is likely to be a mask for unrecognized anger.

If one is not permitted to express anger or even to recognize it within oneself, one is, by simple extension, refused both power and control. Virginia Woolf's *Three Guineas* is an ex-ample of a feminist essay that was universally condemned at its publication because of its anger, its terrible "tone." Brenda Silver, writing of this reaction, asks: "What voice would be 'natural' or 'appropriate' for a woman writing a feminist com-plaint or critique of her culture?" (20). Mary Poovey has re-marked on Caroline Norton's difficulty in finding a proper language or form in her mid-nineteenth-century battle to change the laws governing divorce and child custody (quoted in Silver, 20). Forbidden anger, women could find no voice in which publicly to complain; they took refuge in depression or mad-ness. As Mary Ellmann has pointed out, "the most consistent critical standard applied to women is *shrillness:* blame some-thing written by a woman as *shrill,* praise something as *not shrill*" (in Silver, 13). The other favorite term, of course, is *strident.*

These days the term may be "feminist" *tout court.* Michiko Kakutani, reviewing in the *New York Times* a biography of Margaret Bourke-White by Vicki Goldberg, writes that Bourke-White would, in her profession of photography, "be compelled to break all the conventional expectations for womanly con-duct." But, Kakutani adds, "instead of simply trying to view her subject through the lens of feminist ideology, Ms. Gold-berg judiciously examines the conflicts the photographer ex-perienced herself." Apparently the phrase "feminist ideology" has here taken the place of "shrill" and "strident." I have long puzzled over this remark, and wanted to write Kakutani to ask her what she thought the "lens of feminist ideology" was. I had been trying to define it for years. One thing is clear: if it exists, Goldberg, in her excellent biography, was using it. "Feminist ideology" is another word for trying to understand, in the life of a woman, the life of the mind, which is, as Nancy Miller has noted, "not coldly cerebral but impassioned" (1980, 265).

To denounce women for shrillness and stridency is another way of denying them any right to power. Unfortunately, power is something that women abjure once they perceive the great difference between the lives possible to men and to women, and the violence necessary to men to maintain their position of authority. I have had students walk out of a class when I declared that power is a reasonable subject for discussion. But however unhappy the concept of power and control may make idealistic women, they delude themselves if they believe that the world and the condition of the oppressed can be changed without acknowledging it. Ironically, women who acquire power are more likely to be criticized for it than are the men who have always had it. As Deborah Cameron, an English linguistic theorist, has sardonically observed, male defense of its own power has decreed that nothing "is more ridiculous than a woman who imitates a male activity and is therefore no longer a woman. This can apply not only to speaking and writing, but also to the way a woman looks, the job she does, the way she behaves sexually, the leisure pursuits she engages in, the intellectual activities she prefers and so on *ad infinitum.* Sex differentiation must be rigidly upheld by whatever means are available, for men can be men only if women are unambiguously women" (155–156).

Women of accomplishment, in unconsciously writing their

future lived lives, or, more recently, in trying honestly to deal in written form with lived past lives, have had to confront power and control. Because this has been declared unwomanly, and because many women would prefer (or think they would prefer) a world without evident power or control, women have been deprived of the narratives, or the texts, plots, or examples, by which they might assume power over—take control of—their own lives. The women's movement began, in fact, with discussions of power, powerlessness, and the question of sexual politics. But investigations into the qualities of womanliness have moved away from the point where male power must be analyzed and seen only in relation to female powerlessness. As Myra Jehlen has written, the danger of attempting to find, in this history of female powerlessness, a "female tradition" of autonomy is that, "in the effort to flesh out this vision," one finds that what is depicted is "not actual independence but action despite dependence—and not a self-defined female culture either, but a sub-culture born out of oppression and either stunted or victorious only at often-fatal cost" (581–82). The brutal truth, Jehlen knows, is that "all women must destroy in order to create" (583). "No woman can assume herself because she has yet to create herself, and this the sentimentalists, acceding to their society's definition [of women] did not do" (593). Jehlen understands the hardest fact of all for women to admit and defend: that woman's selfhood, the right to her own story, depends upon her "ability to act in the public domain" (596).

Although feminists early discovered that the private is the public, women's exercise of power and control, and the admission and expression of anger necessary to that exercise, has until recently been declared unacceptable. Yet many of the topics I propose to examine in this book—"unwomanly" ambition, marriage, friendships with women and love for women, aging, female childhood—can be seen accurately only in the light of movements toward *public* power and control. Women need to learn how publicly to declare their right to public power.

The true representation of power is not of a big man beating a smaller man or a woman. Power is the ability to take one's place in whatever discourse is essential to action and the right to have one's part matter. This is true in the Pentagon, in marriage, in friendship, and in politics.

In this book I want to examine how women's lives have been contrived, and how they may be written to make clear, evident, out in the open, those events, decisions, and relationships that have been invisible outside of women's fictions, where literary critics have revealed, in the words of Gilbert and Gubar, "the woman's quest for her own story" (1979, 22). I wish to suggest new ways of writing the lives of women, as biographers, autobiographers, or, in the anticipation of living new lives, as the women themselves.

This is a feminist undertaking. I define *feminist,* using Nancy Miller's words, as the wish "to articulate a self-consciousness about women's identity both as inherited cultural fact and as process of social construction" and to "protest against the available fiction of female becoming." Women's lives, like women's writing, have, in Miller's words, a particularly "vulnerable relation to the culture's central notions of plausibility." It is hard to suppose women can mean or want what we have always been assured they could not possibly mean or want. Miller has shown us how "the literal failure to read women's writing has other theoretical implications." The same may be said of reading women's lives. Unlike the reading of the classics—or of men's lives, or of women's lives as events in the destinies of men—which always include "the frame of *interpretations* that have been elaborated over generations of critical activity," reading women's lives needs to be considered in the absence of "a structure of critical" or biographical commonplaces (129). It all needs to be invented, or discovered, or resaid.

My parents' generation grew up with the Rubáiyát of Omar Khayyám in the Edward FitzGerald version, and so, in time, did I. Its bittersweet flavor of inevitability and wisdom haunted my early years. A much-quoted verse (LXXI) reads:

> The Moving Finger writes; and, having writ,
> Moves on: nor all our Piety nor Wit
> Shall lure it back to cancel half a Line,
> Nor all your Tears wash out a Word of it.

This used to seem evidently, obviously, true. But, at least insofar as women's lives are concerned, it is wrong. Lines can be canceled and washed out; and what the Moving Finger writ may, all along, have been misread. I suggest that it has indeed been misread, and that women have mistakenly supposed themselves deprived of the Piety and Wit certainly sufficient to lure it back.

Feminist criticism, scholarship, and theory have gone further in the last two decades than I, even in my most intense time of hope, could have envisioned. Yet I find myself today profoundly worried about the dissemination of these important new ideas to the general body of women, conscious or unconscious of the need to retell and reencounter their lives. I brood also on the dissensions that have grown among feminist scholars and theoreticians. These divisions, the arguments among scholars about theories, approaches, methodology, are not, of themselves, either dangerous or unexpected. Every new field of knowledge develops these differences. Indeed, they are essential to the progress of understanding. I am certainly not blaming female scholars for failing to maintain a unity men have never achieved, and which is not, in fact, conducive to the flowering of any discipline or to the reorganization of knowledge.

Yet there is a real danger that in rewriting the patriarchal text, scholars will get lost in the intellectual ramifications of their disciplines and fail to reach out to the women whose lives must be rewritten with the aid of the new intellectual constructs. I mean no anti-intellectual complaint here. Without intellectual and theoretical underpinnings, no movement can succeed; the failure of feminism to sustain itself in previous incarnations may well be attributable to its lack of underlying theoretical discourse. But we are in danger of refining the theory and scholarship at the expense of the lives of the women who need to experience the fruits of research.

For this reason, I have chosen to write of women's lives, rather than of the texts I have been trained to analyze and enjoy. I risk a great danger: that I shall bore the theorists and fail to engage the rest, thus losing both audiences. If this does, indeed, occur, I shall at least have failed as the result of a conscious choice, one made in knowledge, insofar as that is ever possible, of the dangers, the challenges, and the vitality whose price is risk.

Safety and closure, which have always been held out to women as the ideals of female destiny, are not places of adventure, or experience, or life. Safety and closure (and enclosure) are, rather, the mirror of the Lady of Shalott. They forbid life to be experienced directly. Lord Peter Wimsey once said that nine-tenths of the law of chivalry was a desire to have all the fun. The same might well be said of patriarchy.

"Men can be men only if women are unambiguously women," Deborah Cameron has written. What does it mean to be unamibiguously a woman? It means to put a man at the center of one's life and to allow to occur only what honors his prime position. Occasionally women have put God or Christ in the place of a man; the results are the same: one's own desires and quests are always secondary. For a short time, during courtship, the illusion is maintained that women, by withholding themselves, are central. Women are allowed this brief period in the limelight—and it is the part of their lives most constantly and vividly enacted in a myriad of representations—to encourage the acceptance of a lifetime of marginality. And courtship itself is, as often as not, an illusion: that is, the woman must entrap the man to ensure herself a center for her life. The rest is aging and regret.

When biographers come to write the life of a woman—and this phenomenon has, of course, occurred with much greater frequency since the advent of contemporary feminism, let us say since the late 1960s—they have had to struggle with the inevitable conflict between the destiny of being unambiguously a woman and the woman subject's palpable desire, or fate, to be something else. Except when writing about queens, biographers of women have not, therefore, been at ease with their subjects—and even with queens, like Elizabeth I of England, there has been a tendency to see them as somewhat abnormal, monstrous. It is no wonder that biographers have largely ignored women as subjects, and that critics of biography have written as though men were the only possible subjects.

If we consider James Clifford's 1962 collection, *Biography as an Art*, we discover there are but six essays out of more than forty that are by women biographers, and that these women wrote about men, or about royal women or women celebrated as events in the lives of famous men. Female biographers, that is, if they wrote about women, chose comfortable subjects whose fame was thrust upon them. Such subjects posed no threaten-

ing questions; their atypical lives provided no disturbing model
for the possible destinies of other women. Catherine Drinker
Bowen, the famous biographer of six men, explains how, when
asked why she had never written about a woman, she did not
dare to respond honestly, "I have, six times." She feared, rightly,
that she would not be understood. Had she been required to
give an explanation, her answer might have been that she wished
to write of daring, extraordinary accomplishment, legal brilliance, and professional fidelity, and what woman subject would
enable her to do that? Moreover, had she found somewhere an
extraordinary woman, how much effort would have been spent
justifying female ambition and describing the landscape of this
unique achievement? Elizabeth Gaskell, until recently the most
salient of female biographers, did not celebrate Charlotte
Brontë's genius, but rescued her from the stigma of being a
famous female writer, an eccentric. Carefully, Gaskell restored
Brontë to the safety of womanliness.

Women writing of their own lives have found it no easier to
detach themselves from the bonds of womanly attitudes. In the
words of Patricia Spacks, writing of eighteenth-century wom-
en's autobiographies, a fantasy of feminine strength, even if it
were achieved, "transformed itself mysteriously into one more
confession of inadequacy. . . . The nature of public and private
selves . . . is for women, in some ways, the reverse of what it
is for men. The face a man turns to the world . . . typically
embodies his strength," while the only acceptable models for
women "involve self-deception and yielding" (1976, 59).

By the time Spacks came, four years later, to publish her
essay entitled "Selves in Hiding," she had extended her observation of women's autobiographical disabilities to our own century. The women whose autobiographies she discusses are
Emmeline Pankhurst, Dorothy Day, Emma Goldman, Eleanor
Roosevelt, and Golda Meir, each a profoundly radical individ-

ual, responsible for revolutionary acts and concepts, and possessing a degree of personal power unusual in men or women. But, Spacks notes, "although each author has significant, sometimes dazzling accomplishments to her credit, the theme of accomplishment rarely dominates the narrative. . . . Indeed to a striking degree they fail directly to emphasize their *own* importance, though writing in a genre which implies self-assertion and self-display." These women accept full blame for any failures in their lives, but shrink from claiming that they either sought the responsibilities they ultimately bore or were in any way ambitious. Day, for example, has what Spacks calls "a clear sense of self—but struggles constantly to lose it." All of these autobiographies "exploit a rhetoric of *uncertainty*" (1980, 113–14). And in all of them the pain of the lives is, like the successes, muted, as though the women were certain of nothing but the necessity of denying both accomplishment and suffering.

All of these modern autobiographies, Spacks observes, "represent a female variant of the high tradition of spiritual autobiography" (1981, 48). One must be called by God or Christ to service in spiritual causes higher than one's own poor self might envision, and authorized by that spiritual call to an achievement and accomplishment in no other way excusable in a female self. So Florence Nightingale, in her desperate desire for an occupation worthy of her talents and desires, four times heard God calling her to his service. But if, for men, spiritual autobiographies tell of personal satisfaction deriving from their spiritual achievement, this is not the case for women. As Mary Mason writes, "Nowhere in women's autobiographies do we find the patterns established by the two prototypical male autobiographers, Augustine and Rousseau; and conversely male writers never take up the archetypal models of Julian, Margery Kemp, Margaret Cavendish, and Anne Bradstreet." On the contrary, Mason writes, "the self-discovery of female identity seems to acknowledge the real presence and recognition of another consciousness, and the disclosure of female self is linked to the identification of some 'other' " (207–8, 210). Identity is grounded through relation to the chosen other. Without such relation, women do not feel able to write openly about themselves; even with it, they do not feel entitled to credit for their own accomplishment, spiritual or not.

Well into the twentieth century, it continued to be impossible for women to admit into their autobiographical narratives the claim of achievement, the admission of ambition, the recognition that accomplishment was neither luck nor the result of the efforts or generosity of others. Jill Conway, in a study of the accomplished women of the Progressive Era in the United States (women born between 1855 and 1865), has remarked upon the narrative flatness with which, in their autobiographies, they have described their exciting lives. Their letters and diaries are usually different, reflecting ambitions and struggles in the public sphere; in their published autobiographies, however, they portray themselves as intuitive, nurturing, passive, but never—in spite of the contrary evidence of their accomplishments—managerial.

The autobiography of Jane Addams, Conway points out, is sentimental and passive: her cause finds *her*, rather than the other way around. Not so in her letters, where she takes over the family business and fights for her due. The money for Hull House, in the autobiography, fell in off the street; her letters reveal the truth. This same pattern, Conway demonstrates, is found in the autobiographies of Ida Tarbell and Charlotte Perkins Gilman. There is a wholly different voice in the letters on the one hand and the autobiographical narratives on the other. All of the autobiographies begin confessionally and, except for Gilman's, report the encounters with what would be the life's work as having occurred by chance. This was, in every case, quite untrue. Each women set out to find her life's work, but the only script insisted that work discover and pursue her, like the conventional romantic lover. As Conway points out, there is no model for the female who is recounting a political narrative. There are no recognizable career stages in such a life, as there would be for a man. Nor do women have a tone of voice in which to speak with authority. As Natalie Davis has said, women up to the eighteenth century could speak with authority only of the family and religion. These women had no models on which to form their lives, nor could they themselves become mentors since they did not tell the truth about their lives.

Ida Tarbell, for example, one of the most famous of the muckrakers, author of the history of the Standard Oil Company, reports that the subject just "happened to be there" and, as Conway shows, credits the idea of her work to others. This is wholly belied by her letters. Where anger is expressed in these autobiographies, it is not, Conway believes, used creatively, as by black male authors. The expression of anger has always been a terrible hurdle in women's personal progress. Above all, the public and private lives cannot be linked, as in male narratives. We hardly expect the career of an accomplished man to be presented as being in fundamental conflict with the demands of his marriage and children; he can allow his public life to expand occasionally into the private sphere without guilt or disorder. These women are therefore unable to write exemplary lives: they do not dare to offer themselves as models, but only as exceptions chosen by destiny or chance.

Much of this has changed since 1970. Many new biographies of women have uncovered new facts or, as Spacks has suggested, sometimes found no significant new facts but only new stories. Some women have always, I believe, looked for new stories, and failed to find them told of women. Now, since about 1970, we have had accounts of lesser lives, great lives, thwarted lives, lives cut short, lives miraculous in their unapplauded achievement. Diane Johnson's *The True History of the First Mrs. Meredith and Other Lesser Lives* was one of the first, followed by biographies of black women, revolutionary women, pioneers, like Margaret Bourke-White, in formerly male professions, and numerous others, some famous, some not. They are all new stories. Only the female life of prime devotion to male destiny had been told before; for the young girl who wanted more from a female biography, there were, before 1970, few or no exemplars.

I can here offer myself as a not atypical example. In the late 1930s and early 1940s I read biographies at the St. Agnes branch of the New York Public Library. In Tom Stoppard's play *Travesties,* one of the characters describes the tastes in poetry of a librarian named Cecily. "Cecily is well bred," he says, "but her views on poetry are very old-fashioned and her knowledge of the poets, as indeed of everything else, is eccentric, being based on alphabetical precedence. She is working her way along the shelves. She has read Allingham, Arnold, Belloc, Blake, both Brownings, Bryon, and so on up to, I believe, B." Thus did I read biography. In my dreams to this day, I stand before the biography shelves at St. Agnes, denying myself an attractive book in *R* because I had reached only *G*. I remember still the opening of the second paragraph of *The Education of Henry Adams,* the volume of my biographical initiation: "Had he been born in Jerusalem under the shadow of the Temple and circumcised in the Synagogue by his uncle the high priest, under the name of Israel Cohen, he would scarcely have been more distinctly branded, and not much more heavily handicapped in the races of the coming century, in running for such stakes as the century was to offer," and my bewilderment before the first of many mysterious allusions based on knowledge and experience I neither had nor seemed likely to acquire. What could possibly be the connection between my ten-year-old self and Henry Adams, born in Boston, compared to an Israel Cohen born in Jerusalem? I was profoundly caught up in biography because it allowed me, as a young girl, to enter the world of daring and achievement. But I had to make myself a boy to enter that world; I could find no comparable biographies of women, indeed, almost no biographies of women at all.

Despite the wonderful biographies we have had in recent years, there still exists little organized sense of what a woman's biography or autobiography should look like. Where should it begin? With her birth, and the disappointment, or reason for no disappointment, that she was not a boy? Do we then slide her into the Freudian family romance, the Oedipal configuration; if not, how do we view the childhood? And now that interest in the pre-Oedipal period has been so vigorously revived by French and American feminists, how closely do we look at that period? What, in short, is the subject's relation—inevitably complex—with her mother? The relation with the father will be less complex, clearer in its emotions and desires, partaking less of either terrible pity or binding love. How does the process of becoming, or failing to become, a sex object operate in the woman's life; how does she cope with the fact that her value is determined by how attractive men find her? If she marries, why does the marriage fail, or succeed? These questions must be answered, not because either the woman or her husband fail or succeed in the familiar roles of wife or husband, but because they have evolved, or failed to evolve, a narrative of marriage that will make possible their development, as individuals and as a couple. What does a "successful" marriage really look like? We have remarkable little evidence of the "story," as opposed to the convention, behind long marriages between women and men who both have established

places in the public sphere. Even less has been told of the life
of the unmarried woman who, consciously or not, has avoided
marriage with an assiduousness little remarked but no less
powerful for being, often, unknown to the woman herself. What
of women friends, of middle age, or of active old age (the years
from sixty to seventy-five)? None of these questions has been
probed within the context of women's as yet unnarrated lives,
lives precisely *not* those that convention, romance, literature,
and drama have, for the most part, given us.

In recent years biography as a genre has come under a good
deal of close scrutiny. Roland Barthes has called biography "a
novel that dare not speak its name," and the understanding
that biographies are fictions, constructions by the biographer
of the story she or he had to tell, has become clear. In all
disciplines, particularly history, scholars have lately written
about how much of what passes as history is in fact evidence
from the prevailing or established opinion of the age under
consideration or, as likely, of the age in which the author of the
history lives. David Bromwich, in an essay on biography, has
observed that "the successful biographies of an age have as
much in common as their biographers rather than as little as
their heroes." In discussing the canonized biographies of Keats,
by Walter Jackson Bate, and of Joyce, by Richard Ellmann,
Bromwich considers why no alternate version of these two
subjects has gained currency. "A modern critic who found Keats
and Joyce interesting because they transmit something other
than the best qualities of the mind would not be expelled from
professional societies. He would simply be seen as entering a
discussion that does not exist. Of this situation the immediate
cause is that criticism has established a certain way of thinking.
But a more remote and more powerful cause is that biography
has made certain facts unthinkable" (167). As Bromwich explains it: "Biographies, after all, define the range of plausible

interpretations of an author." There are three ways, Bromwich continues, in which this definition has worked: "by establishing a consensus about an author's relation to his work, so complete that we are hardly aware of it; by radically altering our picture of an author, and confirming the reputation of his work on a different basis; and by construing an author's work as a transparent apology for his life, with the result that our esteem for the work is diminished and our interest in the life sharpened" (162).

Thus biographies of women had made certain facts unthinkable, and those who wished to expand upon those facts would enter a discussion that, in the academy and the media, did not exist. But what has begun to happen in women's biography since 1970 is that the consensus about the author's relation to her work (if she is a writer) has changed, or is changing; the picture of the author is being altered radically; and often, because of the newness of our experience with the new narratives of women's lives, our interest in the life has sharpened.

Few studies of the last twenty years, and, of course, even fewer in earlier years, have concerned themselves with women's biographies or autobiographies. Where such studies or collections of articles on biography have considered women, they have been the same women: almost always Gertrude Stein, occasionally Margaret Mead. Both of these women might indeed be the subjects of radical new considerations of female biography and autobiography, but in fact they have not been so treated. And in the past, biographies of women were what Phyllis Rose has called "partial biographies":

What I hold against Standard Biographies is not that they are unreadable—the best of them are highly readable—but that they are not, as they pretend to be, impartial. Let me give two examples which are among the most elegant and most readable literary biographies of the recent past: Quentin Bell's *Virginia Woolf* and Gordon Haight's *George*

Eliot. These are good books by any standards. Both are filled with invaluable information. Yet, full as they are, both inevitably leave things out. That is why this kind of biography, which purports to be so fair and objective, is more deceptive than the most flagrantly partisan biography. Quentin Bell leaves out a treatment of Woolf's writing, which is to say he omits much of her inner life apart from her madness, leaving us with the impression of a sick woman who depended extravagantly on a supportive husband. Gordon Haight does not omit accounts of George Eliot's writing to the extent Bell does, but he rarely speculates about her inner life, favoring the done, the said, the written. This gives all the more emphasis to the one theme he allows himself, his one speculation about George Eliot's emotional life, that she needed someone to lean on, that she was not fitted to stand alone. [76–77]

Obviously, Rose admits, she has not picked these examples at random.

Both Bell's biography of Woolf and Haight's of George Eliot are books about women writers by men whose assumptions about women are so deeply assimilated as to have for them the force of truth, self-evident truth. That George Eliot needed someone to lean on is supposed to be a neutral observation. But there is no neutrality. There is only greater or less awareness of one's bias. And if you do not appreciate the force of what you're leaving out, you are not fully in command of what you're doing. [77]

As both Bromwich and Rose perceive, though only Rose considers the particular application to women, biographies of women, if they have been written at all, have been written under the constraints of acceptable discussion, of agreement about what can be left out. And while Bell and Haight (like Bate and Ellmann) have left out a good deal, it must not be assumed that men rather than women, before 1970, necessarily wrote the more constricted biographies of women. On the contrary, if men before 1970 felt the dearth of female subjects, at least they were not personally made anxious by the contemplation of an "outrageous" female destiny. Like Bowen writing about male subjects, men much as Joseph Barry on George Sand and Vincent Sheean on Dorothy Thompson permitted their female adventurers a "quest" plot which, as men, they found familiar. They did not, as female biographers tended to do, feel unbearable discomfort in the face of "unwomanly" lives. The concept of biography itself has changed profoundly in the last two decades, biographies of women especially so. But while biographers of men have been challenged on the "objectivity" of their interpretation, biographers of women have had not only to choose one interpretation over another but, far more difficult, actually to reinvent the lives their subjects led, discovering from what evidence they could find the processes and decisions, the choices and unique pain, that lay beyond the life stories of these women. The choices and pain of the women who did not make a man the center of their lives seemed unique, because there were no models of the lives they wanted to live, no exemplars, no stories. These choices, this pain, those stories, and how they may be more systematically faced, how, in short, one may find the courage to be an "ambiguous woman," are what I want to examine in this book.

One

---

*Women will starve in silence until new
stories are created which confer on them the power
of naming themselves.*

—SANDRA GILBERT AND SUSAN GUBAR

THIS IS the true story of a woman who was born exactly a century before Freud published *The Psychopathology of Everyday Life.*

At the age of four, living on a large estate with horses and space for vigorous activity, she dressed as a boy in order to be able to play more freely. As she grew up, she dressed as a boy for riding and played the male roles opposite conventionally pretty girls in village productions. She found cross-dressing fun, sometimes going to the village near her estate dressed as a young man with her brother who would dress as a girl.

She was married at eighteen to a man of whom Henry James was to observe that he thought he had married an ordinary woman, and found on his hands a (spiritual) sister of Goethe. A year later her first child was born, six years later her second, who was probably not her husband's. By then she had already taken her first lover, years after her husband had taken many mistresses, including her own maid, and behaved brutally toward her. She left her husband eight years after the marriage began and went to live with a lover and collaborator in the nation's capital. Gaining from her husband a separation and an allowance (from her own money), she published two novels and several novelettes under a male pseudonym. Here is her description of how she dressed when she first came to the city:

Above all, I hungered for the theater. I had no illusions that a poor woman could indulge such longings. [They] used to say, "You can't be a woman [here] on under twenty-five thousand." And this paradox, that a woman was not really a woman unless she was smartly dressed, was unbearably hampering to the poor woman artist.

Yet I saw that my young male friends—my childhood companions—were living on as little as I, and knew about everything that could possibly interest young people. The literary and political events, the excitements of the theaters and picture salons, of the clubs and of the streets—they saw it all, they were there. I had legs as strong as theirs, and good feet which had learned to walk sturdily in their great clogs upon the rutted roads of [the country]. Yet on the pavement I was like a boat on ice. My delicate shoes cracked open in two days, my pattens sent me spilling, and I always forgot to lift my dress. I was muddy, tired and runny-nosed, and I watched my shoes and my clothes—not to forget my little velvet hats, which the drainpipes watered—go to rack and ruin with alarming rapidity.

Distressed, she consulted her mother, who said: "When I was young and your father was hard up, he hit on the idea of dressing me as a boy. My sister did the same, and we went everywhere with our husbands: to the theater—oh, anywhere we wanted. And it halved our bills." Here, of course, was the perfect solution. "Having been dressed as a boy in my childhood, and having hunted in knee breeches and shirt, such dress was hardly new to me, and I was not shocked to put it on again." She became famous and had many lovers, including one woman, but she loved one man at a time, and these men were usually younger than she and were not married or the lovers of other women. She liked women, and encouraged younger women all her life. She was the lover and friend of some of the outstanding creative men of her day. She ran a comfortable, hospitable home, eventually delighted in her grandchildren, her garden, conversation, and the possibility of social revolution. Her name, of course, was George Sand.*

To describe her further to you I shall borrow the words of the late Ellen Moers, who in turn calls upon descriptions by Sand's contemporaries to compose this portrait: "She has a brilliant, well-stocked mind and a warm heart; she has courage, energy, vitality, generosity, responsibility, good humor, and charm; she has aristocratic distinction combined with bohemian informality; she is a wise, passionate, down-to-earth human being, and disappointingly sane." Moers continues:

> She was a woman who was a great man: that is what her admirers most wanted to say about George Sand. But words of gender being what they are, suggestions of abnormality and monstrosity cling to their portraits of Sand, all unintentionally and quite the reverse of what her admirers had in mind. Elizabeth Barrett Browning began a sonnet to Sand with the line "Thou large-brained woman and large-hearted man" and what she intended as a tribute to wholeness came out sounding grotesque. Similarly Balzac: "She is boyish, an artist, she is great-hearted, generous, devout, and chaste; she has the main characteristics of a man; ergo, she is not a woman." Similarly Turgenev: "What a brave man she was, and what a good woman." . . . Reading George Sand is to encounter a great man who was all woman. [xv]

And, indeed, if we read her life in any available form, we come again and again to this description of her as both man and woman. She enacted, through lovers and friends, all relationships from mother to master (Flaubert called her "dear master"). She had the power both to give and to receive, to nurture and to be nurtured. Yet all who knew and admired her found themselves without language to describe or address her, without a story, other than her own unique one, in which to encompass her. Although she played every role, including conventionally female ones, although she wrote, in her letters, stereotypically romantic phrases, she did not herself become the victim of these roles or phrases. In one of her novels, the heroine lives dressed as a man, though married and spending intervals in women's clothes; she dies as a man with the word *liberté* on her lips, having said, "I have always felt more than a woman," meaning, of course, more than woman as she is defined.

"Oh you, of the third sex," Flaubert hailed her, and those words that would today sound sneering or disturbing were wholly complimentary then. Flaubert, the ultimate master of words, found it impossible to discover any other way to describe the greatest friend of his life. Henry James, a lifelong admirer of her work, tried many times to describe Sand, and this artist of language and narrative faltered again and again in the attempt. George Sand's, he wrote, was "a method that may be summed up in a fairly simple, if comprehensive statement: it consisted in her dealing with life exactly as if she had been a man—exactly not being too much to say." After her death, James would remark to Flaubert that "the moral of George Sand's tale, the beauty of what she does for us, is not the extension she gives to the feminine nature, but the richness that she adds to the masculine." Flaubert wrote sadly to Turgenev of how at Sand's funeral he had wept "on seeing the coffin pass by." To a woman whose friendship he had shared with Sand, he wrote: "One had to know her as I knew her to realize how much of the feminine there was in that great man, the immensity of tenderness there was in that genius. She will remain one of the radiant splendors of France, unequaled in her glory" (quoted in Barry, 384).

If we compare this story with the now famous account of the probable life of Shakespeare's imagined sister in Virginia Woolf's *A Room of One's Own*, we are moved to explain the miracle that was George Sand's life with the failure of Judith Shakespeare and of so many anonymous women poets. It is easy enough to point to Paris and to French mores for an explanation, but this is not what matters. What matters is that lives do not serve as models; only stories do that. And it is a hard thing to make up stories to live by. We can only retell and live by the stories we have read or heard. We live our lives through texts. They may be read, or chanted, or experienced electronically, or come to us, like the murmurings of our mothers, telling us what conventions demand. Whatever their form or medium, these stories have formed us all; they are what we must use to make new fictions, new narratives.

George Eliot, who did in her life what she could never portray in the lives of her heroines, allowed a minor character in *Daniel Deronda* to protest women's storylessness: "You can never imagine," Daniel's mother tells him, "what it is to have a man's force of genius in you, and yet to suffer the slavery of being a girl. To have a pattern cut out . . . a woman's heart must be of such a size and no larger, else it must be pressed small, like Chinese feet; her happiness is to be made as cakes are, by a fixed receipt."

No careful study of nineteenth-century literature can overlook Sand's tremendous effect on the writers of her time. Hers is the work that explains the Brontës, whose passionate novels lay outside the English tradition, and that goes far to explain the work of Dostoyevski, Whitman, Hawthorne, Matthew Arnold, George Eliot, and many others, to mention only writers who did not meet her but were influenced by her work. Yet few courses in Victorian literature, Russian literature, or American literature even mention George Sand. She and her tremendous influence have disappeared from the canons of French and American literature classes with scarcely a trace. Had she not been a woman, such a disappearance would be inconceivable. But, what is most important, the story of her life has not become an available narrative for women to use in making fictions of their lives. The liberating effect of her novels is greater upon male writers than upon women in England and the United States. The narrative she lived is not yet textually embodied. How may new narratives for women enter texts and then other texts and eventually women's lives?

A few years ago, after having read many exciting new biographies of women, I had a shocking experience in going through Peter Ackroyd's biography of T. S. Eliot. I had felt obliged to read it as part of my professional duties, as my special field is modern British literature. And the old sense rushed over me of the ease of male lives, that sense I had so long lived with—for I have been teaching modern British literature for twenty-five years. I fell into this biography like one who hears again the stories of her youth. Here was a life for which there was indeed not only *the* narrative, but so many possible narratives. Despite Eliot's egregious sexual and personal failures, despite professional uncertainties, writing blocks, and frightening social judgments, despite his confused national, religious, and marital loyalties, his story reads as easily, as inevitably, as those of the Hardy boys.

For the first time in years I came to realize how far in my search for women's lives and texts I had moved from this wonderful banquet of possible quests, conceivable stories, available narrations. I settled into this biography—which is very well written, by the way—as easily as women, if one were to believe the advertisements, settle into harlequin romances. I read the story as romances are read because I knew how it would come out, knew that, of all the choices life might offer

him, Eliot would find those that suited. Yet romances, which
end when the woman is married at a very young age, are the
only stories for women that end with the sense of peace, all
passion spent, that we find in the lives of men. I have read
many moving lives of women, but they are painful, the price is
high, the anxiety is intense, because there is no script to follow,
no story portraying how one is to act, let alone any alternative
stories.

Ackroyd writes of Eliot that "he could not work easily [on
the play *Samson Agonistes*] because there was no literary context for such writing from which to draw energy or inspiration."
He had "complained to Virginia Woolf that, in the absence of
illustrious models, the contemporary writer was compelled to
work on his own." One smiles at what must have passed through
her mind as she heard this. Ackroyd continues: "Throughout
[Eliot's published work] there is evidence of an imagination
which received with full force the impression of others writers'
forms and language, and which was then able to assimilate
them within an original design. He always needed a safety net,
as it were, before he indulged in his own acrobatics" (147). It
is precisely such a safety net that is absent from women's lives,
let alone their writings. How are they to imagine forms and
language they have never heard? How are they to live to write,
and to write that other women may live? There was always,
Ackroyd tells us, a moment of "despair" during Eliot's creation
of a work. For Virginia Woolf, of course, there was all to do
from the beginning, and enough despair to have discouraged
women for generations.

Ackroyd writes that "only in response to other poetry . . .
could Eliot express his deepest feelings" (149). For women,
that response has almost always been to the poetry of men, to
a point of view not theirs, often, as with Eliot, deliberately
excluding them. In *The Wasteland* only the silent hyacinth girl

is acceptable, neither loathsome nor destructive—and it is her silence he treasures. Ackroyd says that "the anonymous role of a *Times* reviewer in fact suited [Eliot] very well: it allowed him to adopt the role of the scholar, and thus employ the tone of established authority" (97). Virginia Woolf, who also reviewed for the *Times*, must have liked the anonymous role at first; anonymity eases women's pains, alleviates the anxiety about the appropriateness of gender. As Charlotte Brontë was to write to her publisher, "I am neither a man nor a woman but an author," and Cynthia Ozick and Joyce Carol Oates have said much the same in our day. But had Woolf employed the tone of established authority, she would have denied her life's experience. There is no "objective" or universal tone in literature, for however long we have been told there is. There is only the white, middle-class, male tone.

But the question is not only one of narrative and tone, it is also one of language. How can women create stories of women's lives if they have only male language with which to do it? The question, in Mary Jacobus's words, is "the nature of women's access to culture and their entry into literary discourse. The demand for education provides the emancipatory thrust of much nineteenth and twentieth century feminism. . . . But this access to a male-dominated culture may equally be felt to bring with it alienation, repression, division—a silencing of the 'feminine,' a loss of women's inheritance. . . . To propose a difference of view, a difference of standard—to begin to ask what the difference might be—is to call in question the very terms which constitute that difference." Jacobus speaks of "the rift experienced by women writers in a patriarchal society, where language itself may reinscribe the structures by which they are oppressed." The "demand for an impossible desire" can condemn women to silence even when their entry to edu-

cation and the professions seems to have permitted them ut-
terance.

The problem, again in Jacobus's words, is this: "Women's
access to discourse involves submission to phallocentricity, to
the masculine and the symbolic: refusal, on the other hand,
risks reinscribing the feminine as a yet more marginal madness
or nonsense." Refusal in this sense for French philosopher
Julia Kristeva involves a refusal of the symbolic, the Law of the
Father, that would locate women within the realm of the semi-
otic, "the pre-Oedipal phase of rhythmic onomatopoeic babble
which precedes the Symbolic but remains inscribed in those
[early] pleasurable and rupturing aspects of language." Woman
is thus offered, on the one hand, exclusion from (patriarchal)
language itself or, on the other, a circumscription within the
feminine domain of language, a domain that "in fact marks the
place of women's oppression and confinement." What to do?
Jacobus suggests that, "though necessarily working within 'male'
discourse," we women "work ceaselessly to deconstruct it: to
write what cannot be written" (10–21). As Jimmy Durante put
it, thems the conditions that pervail.

What have women done about it? Here is Margaret Homans's summary of where we are: "The French writers who
accept the premise that language and experience are coexten-
sive also understand language to be a male construct whose
operation depends on women's silence and absence, so that
when women write they do not represent themselves as women.
In contrast, most recent feminist criticism in this country has
pragmatically assumed that experience is separable from language and thus that women are or can be in control of language
rather than controlled by it" (186). To put it differently, as
Elaine Marks does, American feminist critics see women as
oppressed by sexism, "their voices unheard within the domi-

nant culture," whereas for French critics, women are *repressed*, equivalent to the unconscious, and therefore not representable in language (55).

What it comes down to is this (in Homans's words): "There is a specifically gender-based alienation from language that is characterized by the special ambiguity of women's simultaneous participation in and exclusion from [the male] hegemonic group." Or (in Jacobus's words): "Can women adapt traditionally male-dominated modes of writing to the articulation of female oppression and desire?" Or (in my words): How can we find narratives of female plots, stories that will affect other stories and, eventually, lives, that will cause us neither to bury Shakespeare's sister nor to throw up our hands in describing George Sand because we are unwilling to call her either a woman (under the old plot) or a man when she isn't one?

In a recent seminar entitled "Gender and Literature" offered to Columbia University Master's students, we read, among much else, four stories of women who, feeling trapped in a script they did not write but were slowly beginning to analyze, look about them for a way out, a way on to a different life: "The Awakening" by Kate Chopin, "To Room 19" by Doris Lessing, "A Jury of Her Peers," by Susan Glaspell, and a brilliant but lesser-known story by Jean Stubbs, "Cousin Lewis." What the class came to see was not alone the gender arrangements, the appropriate behavior, that had confined these women in stories that had always been assumed to be intelligent and fair; they also saw the absence of any narrative that could take the women past their moment of revelation and support their bid for freedom from the assigned script. Various dramatic events await these women as they strive to break free, or to satisfy a longing for identity and psychic space: suicide in two cases, murder in one, a more confined marriage in the fourth, "Cousin Lewis," where a woman who donned male clothing to tell her children stories of adventure is declared unfit to raise her children. The class remembered that, in addition, we had read Hawthorne's *The Scarlet Letter* and Cather's *O Pioneers!* In both of these novels the woman had lived through her special destiny but left no path behind her for future women, had lived with no community of women, no sense of bonding with other women. Not only had these women no stories other than their refusal of the plot in which most women lived, and no women with whom to talk of what they had themselves learned, but they would have been hard put to answer the inevitable question asked of unhappy women: What do you want?

If I had to emphasize the lack either of narrative or of language to the formation of new women's lives, I would unquestionably emphasize narrative. Much, of a profound and perceptive nature, has been written about the problem of women coping with male language that will not say what they wish: we remember Woolf's enigmatic statement that Jane Austen was the first to write a woman's sentence. Some part of us responds to this, as to the words of Anne Elliot in *Persuasion*—"Men have had every advantage of us in telling their story. Education has been theirs in so much higher a degree; the pen has been in their hands."—and of Bathsheba in Thomas Hardy's *Far from the Madding Crowd*—"It is difficult for a woman to define her feelings in language which is chiefly made by men to express theirs." But what we speak of here, as I suspect Homans and Jacobus also do, is not so much women's lack of a language as their failure to speak profoundly to one another. As Deborah Cameron has written, "Men do not control meaning at all. Rather women *elect* to use modes of expression men can understand because that is the best way of getting men to listen" (105). The problem, she asserts, is one not of language but of power. And power consists to a large extent in deciding what stories will be told; in Bromwich's (slightly altered) words, male power has made certain stories unthinkable.

As Cameron perceives, women's talk is not inherently or naturally subversive; it becomes so when women begin "to privilege it over their interactions with men (as in consciousness-raising groups). Men trivialize the talk of women not because they are afraid of any such talk, but in order to make women themselves downgrade it." Women's talk will indeed be harmless as long as women consider it trivial compared to talk with men (157–58).

Women must turn to one another for stories; they must share the stories of their lives and their hopes and their unacceptable fantasies. Sartre, in the introduction to his biography of Jean Genet, has defined the story as "freedom confronted by fate, first crushed by misfortunes, then turning against them and gradually controlling them." Genius, he sets out to prove, is "not a gift, but rather the way one invents in desperate situations," and in considering it we must "retrace in detail the history of a liberation" (quoted in Sarde, 8). We have seen that even our women geniuses, and the biographers of women geniuses, do not "retrace in detail the history of a liberation." Rather, even women geniuses do not have their efforts recorded as inventions "in desperate situations." What then of the rest of us?

We must stop reinscribing male words, and rewrite our ideas about what Nancy Miller calls a female impulse to power, as opposed to the erotic impulse which alone is supposed to impel women. We know we are without a text, and must discover one. Virginia Woolf speaks of George Eliot's heroines' "demand for something—they scarcely know what—for something that is perhaps incompatible with the facts of human existence." That is the something women need to reinscribe. As Miller writes, "the plots of women's literature are not about 'life'. . . . They are about the plots of literature itself, about the constraints . . . of rendering a female life in fiction." The reinscriptions of "experience . . . in literature are organizations, when they are not fantasies, of the dominant"—that is, the male—culture. Literature does not write our, women's, "fictions of desire" (43, 44).

How might it do so? In *Alice Doesn't: Feminism, Semiotics, Cinema,* Teresa de Lauretis concludes by identifying "consciousness raising" as a way to appropriate reality: "The fact that today the expression consciousness raising has become dated and more than slightly unpleasant, as any word will that has been appropriated, diluted, digested and spewed out by the media, does not diminish the social and subjective impact of a practice—the collective articulation of one's experience of sexuality and gender—which has produced, and continues to elaborate, a radically new mode of understanding the subject's relation to social-historical reality. Consciousness raising is the original critical instrument that women have developed toward such understanding, the analysis of social reality, and its critical revision." What she is recommending is the "practice of self-consciousness," the "political, theoretical, self-analyzing practice by which the relations of the subject in social reality can be rearticulated from the historical experience of women" (186). To put it simply, we must begin to tell the truth, in groups, to one another. Modern feminism began that way, and we have lost, through shame or fear of ridicule, that important collective phenomenon.

Consciousness raising, as far as it went, revealed to the white, middle-class women who took part in it that, isolated in nuclear families, they suffered individual guilt, each supposing herself a monster when she did not fit the acceptable narrative of a female life. It is questionable how much any individual woman before the women's movement was helped by individual therapy or advice. What became essential was for women to see themselves collectively, not individually, not caught in some individual erotic and familial plot and, inevitably, found wanting. Individual stories from biographies and autobiographies have always been conceived of as individual, eccentric lives. I suspect that female narratives will be found where women exchange stories, where they read and talk collectively of ambitions, and possibilities, and accomplishments.

I do not believe that new stories will find their way into texts if they do not begin in oral exchanges among women in groups hearing and talking to one another. As long as women are isolated one from the other, not allowed to offer other women the most personal accounts of their lives, they will not be part of any narrative of their own. Like Penelope awaiting Ulysses, weaving and unweaving, women will be staving off destiny and not inviting or inventing or controlling it. They will live their lives individually, among the suitors, without a story to be told, wondering whether or when to marry. In the *Odyssey*, it is important that Athena appears to Penelope in a dream as her sister, whom Penelope has not seen since her marriage. What other woman might Athena have impersonated? There were no other women peers in Penelope's life, certainly none near her. One of the reasons Samuel Butler thought the *Odyssey* had been written by a woman was because " when Ulysses and Penelope are in bed and are telling their stories to one another, Penelope tells hers first. I believe a male writer would have made Ulysses's story come first, and Penelope's second" (quoted in Weigle, 204). It does not occur to Butler that Penelope, never the subject, like her husband, of individual narrative, has new stories to tell. But we must note that Penelope has no one other than her husband to whom to tell her stories, and only husbands who have been absent for twenty years could be expected to listen with such attention, and to listen first. Even in more recent literature, we see how alone women are, how without close women friends are Jane Austen's heroines, and Charlotte Brontë's, and George Eliot's.

There will be narratives of female lives only when women no longer live their lives isolated in the houses and the stories of men.

Two

Life robbed [Dorothy Sayers] of most of
the ordinary human experiences of satisfactory
emotional relationships, sexual and parental. No
wonder she had to fall back on the intellect.

—JAMES BRABAZON

NINA AUERBACH HAS WRITTEN a single sentence about George Eliot that should be engraved upon the forehead of every biographer of what Shaw called an unwomanly woman: "Whether deliberately, unconsciously, or accidentally, she seems to have composed her own life so that its fitful, rudderless, and self-doubting first half was alchemized into gold when the austere bluestocking became the fallen woman" (1982, 183). Auberbach has, with dazzling succinctness, identified a phenomenon evident in the lives of accomplished women who live in a storyless time and are either trapped in, or have wasted energy opposing, the only narrative available to them: the conventional marriage or erotic plot. For women who wish to live a quest plot, as men's stories allow, indeed encourage, them to do, some event must be invented to transform their lives, all unconsciously, apparently "accidentally," from a conventional to an eccentric story. George Eliot took herself abruptly out of the conventional plot by committing herself to live, as if in marriage, with George Henry Lewes, who could not divorce his legal wife. It was a relationship utterly abhorrent to Victorian morality. By one outrageous act she escaped social demands, the compulsion to motherhood, and despair at her lack of accepted sex appeal; by the same act she satisfied her sexual desires, her need for a certain dependency, and, above all, her need for space in which to work.

So many women have done, though often in ways less immediately obvious than Eliot's. In our own time of many possible life patterns, it is difficult to grasp how absolutely women of an earlier age could expel themselves from conventional society (that is, all society) by committing a social, usually a sexual, sin. The lives of women who died before the middle of the twentieth century should always be carefully examined for such an act, which would usually (but not always) occur in a woman's late twenties or thirties. Here, as with other aspects of female lives, it is well to remember that life crises that have been identified as patterns in male lives often occur at a later age in women.

Erik Erikson has identified a period known as the *moratorium* but, as with all Erikson's writing, only the male is seen as the model for human development. Nonetheless, his description of the moratorium is highly useful in looking at women's lives. In the lives of certain gifted men, Erikson writes—George Bernard Shaw and William James are excellent examples—there is a time when the individual appears, before the age of thirty, to be getting nowhere, accomplishing none of his aims, or altogether unclear as to what those aims might be. Such a person is, of course, actually preparing for the task that, all unrecognized, awaits. For my purposes, Yeats is a clearer example of the opposition that appears between what an individual seems to want and what he or she in fact does to facilitate the as yet unrealized vocation. Yeats, not unlike George Eliot, might have dismally seen himself as without work, sexual experience, or daily companionship. Before Erikson, we would have been inclined to search for psychological restraints upon male sexual expression in a situation such as that in which Yeats found himself. It is, however, likelier that Yeats was providing himself with an experience essential to the poet he sought to become, and that he lived the life suited to his vocation rather than to what he consciously recorded as his desires. He loved an unattainable woman because that love, and his unquenched desire, sharpened him for poetry.

Dorothy L. Sayers, a scholar of medieval literature who earned a first-class degree in French at Oxford, the author of remarkably popular detective novels featuring Lord Peter Wimsey, and, later, Harriet Vane, offers a clear biographical example of the female moratorium and the unconscious decision to place one's life outside the bounds of society's restraints and ready-made narratives. Sayers's life was written by James Brabazon; it was a life I had hoped to write, and might have written, but the choice of Brabazon by Sayers's executors was in important ways a wise one. He had two qualifications essential for the writing of her biography: he is English, with that inherent understanding of a culture that cannot be learned; and he is conversant with and sympathetic to Sayers's religious beliefs. I enter into dialogue with his biography in behalf of those qualities I can add: an understanding of women whose lives include risk and the desire for individual achievement in the public world, as well as, or in place of, marital love.

There is, of course, danger in the writing of every biography, which is why Roland Barthes has written that he finds biography offensive because it entails "a counterfeit integration of the subject." Who can deny it? In choosing among biographers and biographies, we choose among counterfeit integrations. Perhaps in choosing the lives we lead, we do the same.

Let any woman imagine for a moment a biography of herself based upon those records she has left, those memories fresh in the minds of surviving friends, those letters that chanced to be kept, those impressions made, perhaps, on the biographer who was casually met in the subject's later years. What secrets, what virtues, what passions, what discipline, what quarrels would, on the subject's death, be lost forever? How much would have vanished or been distorted or changed, even in our memories? We tell ourselves stories of our past, make fictions or stories of it, and these narrations *become* the past, the only part of our lives that is not submerged.

James Brabazon, like all biographers, had to form his biography from what remained. But he formed it also from his own interpretation of what a woman's life can be. I have a different story (or version) of her life; I believe Sayers's life to be an excellent example of a woman's unconscious "fall" into a condition where vocation is possible and out of the marriage plot that demands not only that a woman marry but that the marriage and its progeny be her life's absolute and only center.

It is impossible to overestimate the importance of her detective novels in my own life during what should have been, but was not, a time of hope—a phrase, significantly, that was used by C. P. Snow to characterize a man's youth, when all seems possible and his destiny awaits him if he will but set his feet upon the path. For the young woman, however, for whom the female destiny of flirtation, wedding, and motherhood is insufficient or even unattractive, youth is less a time of hope than a time of uncertainty, at worst a time of depression and some wild experimentation among the passions: as though, in watching male passions turned upon oneself, one could distract one's attention from the blunted female destiny. In such a time, I read Sayers, and through her wit, her intelligence, her portrayal of a female community and a moral universe, I caught sight of a possible life. (On the occasion of the fiftieth anniversary of the publication of her *Gaudy Night*, I addressed a conference at Somerville College, Oxford, celebrating the event, and tried to suggest what that novel had meant over the years to its American women readers.) Sayers provided a fantasy, of course—all detective novels are fantasies—but at least hers was not the romantic fantasy long prescribed for women.

James Brabazon has noticed little of this. He begins his biography not with Sayers's birth but with her sense of despair at the age of twenty-eight, when she was, in Brabazon's words, "a virgin and unemployed." Brabazon puts the virginity first, but Sayers herself, writing to her parents, complains: "I can't find the work I want." In the list of deprivations that follows, she mentions money, clothes, and a holiday—all before a man. "For the most part," Brabazon writes, Sayers "made the best—and a very good best—of the cards that were dealt her." He suspects that Sayers might have been happier had she been pretty, "normally" married, with lots of children, and had she not been a lonely, only child. He reads her life as a "fall[ing] back on the intellect" when the cards dealt her failed to include the chance to be a wife and mother. He assumes that Sayers had "a raw deal" in not being "physically attractive and sure of herself in adolescence." In short, he notes that Sayers lacked the necessary accoutrements for the successful enactment of a male-designed script. He recognizes, but does not endorse, the possibility that it is precisely not having been sexually attractive in youth that enables women to develop the ego-strength to be creative and ultimately part of the instrumental rather than the expressive world in adulthood. What Brabazon failed to recognize is that Sayers's youth is an example of the moratorium: with highly gifted women, as with men, the failure to lead the conventional life, to find the conventional way early, may signify more than having been dealt a poor hand of cards. It may well be the forming of a life in the service of a talent felt, but unrecognized and unnamed. This condition is marked by a profound sense of vocation, with no idea of what that vocation is, and by a strong sense of inadequacy and deprivation.

We can sense now that it was essential to Sayers's sense of vocation that she (like George Eliot) put beyond reach the temptation of the conventional woman's life. By becoming pregnant as an unmarried woman at a time when that was (as it was to remain in Sayers's mind always) a great sin, by pouring out her love to a man (not the father of her child) who was incapable of receiving it, Sayers assured herself her strange independence. The letters that remain from her to John Cournos, the man she so unaccountably loved and lost, are particularly revealing of both her despair and the hints she seemed to catch of the possibilities that lay ahead. John Cournos, a Russian Jew whom she passionately desired, left her for a wealthier woman, and it was to him she wrote of her pregnancy and of the affair with another man. Brabazon is correct in discerning in Sayers a great desire for sexual experience: she wished not only to be desired but to experience orgasm. With the largely unsatisfactory man who eventually became her husband, Sayers found both sexual satisfaction and independence. That Sayers's husband, Oswald Atherton Fleming ("Mac"), had been psychologically damaged in World War I made for his unhappiness but not hers, in a profound sense. We may even surmise that his refusal to allow her child to live with them suited, at some unconscious level, her own needs. Fulfilling the role society has assigned to the male more than Mac did, Sayers paid for her son's care, supervised his education, and went about her work. Brabazon cleverly guesses that Mac, whatever his failings, was, at least in the early years of their marriage, good in bed.

Sayers's attitude toward her appearance in her later years confirms the sense that, once her moratorium had passed, she was free to disdain those efforts of dress, cosmetics, and hairdressing that had always caused her undue effort and dissatisfaction. The sense of conforming to the ideals of attractive womanhood is one that sustains many women in our culture as they grow older. To "let oneself go" is to resign one's sense of oneself as a woman and therefore, in many cases, as a person. (We remember that Virginia Woolf said of Ella Wheeler Wilcox: "Rather than look like a bluestocking she would have forsaken literature altogether.") Women are, of course, encouraged to be concerned with their physical attractiveness; for that reason it requires great courage to ignore one's appearance and reach out, as it were, from behind it to attract and spellbind: it also requires great talent. Ralph Hone has quoted in his biography (Brabazon does not) Mary Ellen Chase's account of Sayers's appearance in 1934, when she was forty-one:

There can be few plainer women on earth than Dorothy Sayers, and the adjective is an extremely kind one. She seemingly had no neck at all. Her head appeared to be closely joined to the regions between her shoulder blades in back and her collar bone in front. She had a florid complexion, very blue, near-sighted eyes, and wore glasses which quivered. Her thinning hair rarely showed evidence of care or forethought in its total lack of arrangement. . . . She was large, rawboned, and awkward. [79]

Yet Chase, a woman frightened of unconventionality but recognizing, perhaps even envying, the sheer guts Sayers needed to be so emphatically herself, adds: "Just as I have never seen a less attractive woman to look upon, I have never come across one so magnetic to listen to." There were times when Sayers, even in the late years, got herself up to look quite handsome. But can it be doubted that for a woman to grow fat in middle age is to dissociate her personhood from her feminine appeal?

(We may note in this connection that recent, highly sympathetic biographers of Elizabeth Cady Stanton and Margaret Mead deplore and fail to understand the large size of their subjects in old age.) As Sayers was to write about women wearing trousers, answering men who criticized this unbecoming practice: "If the trousers do not attract you, so much the worse; for the moment I do not want to attract you. I want to enjoy myself as a human being."

All the same, one must be careful, as some writers on Sayers have not been, to recognize that she was not unattractive in her youth. Brabazon indicates that if she never stood out as a sex object, she had plenty of vitality and appeal, and received offers of marriage. She had a slender neck in those days, and was "long and slim." What she wanted then was "a man to her measure," someone she could fight with and intimidate. Of course, she found no such man who would have enabled her, she said, to "put a torch to the world." Instead, she put a torch to the world by inventing him.

Only when the character of Lord Peter Wimsey was well established could she, like the Old Testament God, create a woman. The fictional Harriet Vane has much in common with Sayers, most of all devotion to her work and the intelligent woman's inability to find a man worthy of her love. In writing *Gaudy Night*, therefore, in which Peter and Harriet agree to marry, Sayers produced the novel she had prepared all her life to write. She had completed her task of transforming the detective story and embodying her vision of intellectual integrity in a woman character.

Alas, Sayers's eventual destiny for Harriet Vane is characteristic of women writers' failure or reluctance to create women characters with as much autonomy as they themselves possess. Sayers is certainly better than George Eliot in this respect: Eliot failed to move any of her women protagonists out of the confined female world. But it tells us much about the problems of women's lives, and of writing about them, to notice that, having created Harriet Vane, Sayers faltered in sustaining the character. Nor could she even abandon Harriet, as she did Peter, to a continued career of work and autonomy. Instead, Sayers can be seen to have invented Harriet Vane as a kind of token woman, and then married her off.

Sayers has told us at considerable length about her creation of Peter Wimsey and of his ultimate refinement; how she had intended to get rid of him but was unable to because, just as she lifted the ax, the public began to flock around in their admiring millions. We are, however, rather left to infer that Harriet Vane, having served "in the conventional Perseus manner" as a maiden to be rescued by the ever more popular Lord Peter, was neither created nor done away with as the result of any particular forethought. It was only Peter who was to be made into a "complete human being" or to be married off and got rid of.

Sayers confesses that she could not at once "marry Peter off to the young woman he had . . . rescued from death and infamy, because I could find no form of words in which she could accept him without loss of self-respect." Sayers cleverly neglects to mention, or perhaps never recognized, that the complete human being she was creating was Harriet Vane. However well she may have hidden her need to write about Harriet, Sayers was primarily compelled not to make Peter more human, but to create a woman—autonomous, intellectual, unwomanly, and, ultimately, lovable. It was Harriet who, once presented in all her amazing autonomy, could then be married off and done away with. Sayers says she did not do away with Peter because "a lingering instinct of self-preservation, and the deterrent object-lesson of Mr. Holmes's rather scrambling return from the Reichenbach Falls, prevented me from actually killing and burying the nuisance." This is pure camouflage, pure pulling of the wool over her eyes and ours. Once Harriet's independent role and character had been fully played out, Sayers put her back into the proper womanly, wifely position in *Busman's Honeymoon* and abandoned her to the fate of a married woman, a fate delineated further in the short story "Talboys." Peter, meanwhile, returned as the detective he had always been, diverting himself in detection even during his honeymoon and even during Harriet's childbirth scene. Sayers's need to create a wholly independent woman had been happily assuaged.

Let us take a harder look at Harriet Vane. Here is a woman who has, metaphorically speaking, killed and abandoned her lover when she outgrew him. So realistic, so "unfeminine" is her scorn of him that she is tried for his literal murder in *Strong Poison*, a fate society might well mete out to a woman who treats a man as men have ever treated their women lovers. Peter, that ideal man, recognizes her right to have had a lover as equal to his own (a far from common view at that time), and rescues her, not so much from the charge of murder as from the charge of unwomanly conduct. She cannot accept him in his Perseus role, and proceeds—in what may be the most extraordinary, because uncritical, portrait of an independent woman in all literature—to enact her belief that "the best remedy for a bruised heart is not, as so many people seem to think, repose upon a manly bosom. Much more efficacious are honest work, physical activity, and the sudden acquisition of wealth." Because Sayers's readers anticipated romance and the inevitable abandonment of this declared independence, they failed to be shocked by how unusual Harriet was. She travels alone, is not given to "groupy" activities at Oxford, and works there, independently, not only as a detective but as a member of a rare community of female scholars and colleagues who are, no

more than she, refugees from a male bosom. In all the novels
in which she appears, furthermore, she fairly flaunts her independence, scorns women who flutter around gigolos or otherwise bother much with men, and befriends women so
independent that they might even be seen as outside the marriage game altogether. Harriet, indeed, cannot be sentimental
enough to like someone because she once did, or because the
person is ill, and she is a bundle of arrogant and wholly defensible opinions. *And* without ever discussing the pros and cons,
she dines alone in restaurants though the propriety of doing so
is even today deemed worthy of debate in New York's leading
newspaper.

Dorothy L. Sayers, who invented an extraordinary life for
herself, needed, I am certain, to create once and for all a woman
as independent and, in the light of proper womanly behavior,
as outrageous as she. But once having written Harriet Vane
out, Sayers had to get rid of her. Having invented such a character was unusual enough; to sustain her would have required
a miracle. Women's stories always end with marriage, with
wifedom and motherhood; thus it was with Harriet. The tale
about killing off Peter was folderol. Sayers didn't want to kill
him off; that was her excuse to herself and others for creating
Harriet. Then, that done, and Harriet disposed of, Sayers could
go on to other work which Peter's earnings ("the sudden acquisition of wealth") enabled her to do.

As Sayers grew older and more famous, she moved more
and more into that "other work," the study of Christianity,
which she found compelling. The importance of much of Sayers's writing on religion and on medieval subjects is indisputa-
ble. Yet Brabazon is surely right in asserting that it is for the
creation of Lord Peter Wimsey, and the novels and stories in
which he appears, that Sayers will be longest remembered.
The Wimsey books will endure for all the reasons books do

endure: above all, because they give pleasure and because, beneath their glittering surfaces, they question the society they portray. It is easier to be an apologist for a society than a subtle subverter of it. Yet for all that, Sayers's adventure in middle age into different kind of work marks her yet again as a woman whose life follows a pattern rarely perceived. Her early "fall" permitted her the life she could not consciously, against the weight of societal expectations, choose for herself. Her change of direction in middle age marks that often radical shift, either in work or in emphasis, that some women, up to then unconsciously courageous, consciously make in their later years. Sayers's writings about Wimsey, like Woolf's writings of the 1920s, may continue to be the most popular, the most cherished of her works. But the courage and importance of the later change must not, for that reason, be underestimated or dismissed as inferior or less worthy.

In 1943, Sayers turned down a Lambeth Degree, a rare honor bestowed by the Archbishop of Canterbury, who offered her a Doctorate of Divinity. Because her letters to the archbishop have not been released, Brabazon can only guess at her reasons for refusing this great honor, but his guess is a sound one: she was aware of the sinfulness of her son's birth, and afraid that this fact might be ferreted out. We, who now know all the facts, may well decide that it was in her sinfulness, rather than in her devoutness, that her true destiny as a woman is revealed. Certainly her life, both in its unwritten, unconscious story and in its final turn toward the medieval and Christian studies that had always intrigued her, teaches us about the possible hidden lives of accomplished women who were educated enough to have had a choice and brave enough to have made one.

Three

---

*When Sleeping Beauty wakes up
she is almost fifty years old.*

—MAXINE KUMIN

*O*NLY IN THE LAST THIRD OF the twentieth century have women broken through to a realization of the narratives that have been controlling their lives. Women poets of one generation—those born between 1923 and 1932—can now be seen to have transformed the autobiographies of women's lives, to have expressed, and suffered for expressing, what women had not earlier been allowed to say. The constraints on women's writing the truth about their lives were lifted first by women poets, sometimes in their poetry, sometimes in essays, books, and interviews. These women, all of them middle class and white, simultaneously dismantled the past and reimagined the future. They found a way to recognize and express their anger; harder still, they managed to bear, for a time at least, the anger in men that their work aroused.

Had I been writing about fiction, and the outstanding examples of new narratives of women's lives available there, I would have had to write chiefly about the works of black women writers. The novelists Toni Morrison and Alice Walker, among others, have more profoundly and dazzlingly discovered new narratives for women, and new ways of understanding old nar-

ratives, than any other contemporaries I can name. My decision not to examine fiction in this book excludes analyses of
their novels, but the brilliant criticism already written and
being written on them excuses me here, as it has in the discussion of other fictions. What it is important to note for my purpose is the difference between the lives of "my" generation of
poets and the lives of black women. Toni Morrison enunciates
this with great clarity:

> It seems to me there's an enormous difference in the writing of
> black and white women. Aggression is not as new to black women as
> it is to white women. Black women seem able to combine the nest
> and the adventure. They don't see conflicts in certain areas as do
> white women. They are both safe harbor and ship; they are both inn
> and trail. We, black women, do both. We don't find these places,
> these roles, mutually exclusive. That's one of the differences. White
> women often find if they leave their husbands and go out into the
> world, it's an extraordinary event. If they've settled for the benefits
> of housewifery that preclude a career, then it's marriage *or* a career
> for them, not both, not *and*. [122]

Morrison has remarked that "it's not so much that women
write differently from men, but that black women write differently from white women. Black men don't write very differently from white men" (122). I think that in the generation
born between 1923 and 1932, white women began to write
more differently from white men in ceasing to accept the place
to which white men had assigned them. Elizabeth Fox-
Genovese has observed the "gap between black women and
the dominant [white] model of womanhood" (176), but that gap
is likely, in future years, to be less obvious because of the
changes in white women's ideas about womanhood.

The generation of white women poets I refer to lived through
World War II (as I did). Jane Cooper, born in 1924, sets it for
us: "World War II was the war I grew up into. I was fourteen

when England and France declared war on Germany; I was
seventeen at the time of Pearl Harbor; the first atomic bombs
were dropped on Hiroshima and Nagasaki, and peace treaties
were signed, just before my senior year in college" (33). For
most of us, the men we loved and/or married were of the
generation that fought in that war. And here, in a stanza, Maxine Kumin describes those war years in retrospect, exactly as I
remember them:

> She
> remembers especially a snapshot
> of herself in a checked gingham outfit.
> He is wearing his Navy dress whites.
> She remembers the illicit weekend
> in El Paso, twenty years before
> illicit weekends came out of the closet.
> Just before Hiroshima
> just before Nagasaki
> they nervously straddled the border
> he an ensign on a forged three-day pass
> she a technical virgin from Boston.
> What he remembers is vaster:
> something about his whole future
> compressed to a stolen weekend.
> He was to be shipped out tomorrow
> for the massive land intervention.
> He was to have stormed Japan.
> Then, merely thinking of dying
> gave him a noble erection.

It is in the same poem, "The Archeology of a Marriage,"
that Kumin writes what appears in the epigraph to this chapter:
"When Sleeping Beauty wakes up / she is almost fifty years
old." That's a slight exaggeration—such is the way of poets—
but it does indicate that these poets were at middle age, if they
were not yet fifty, when they began their marvelous disman-

tling. These poets, all American, are (in the order of their birth): Denise Levertov, Jane Cooper, Carolyn Kizer, Maxine Kumin, Anne Sexton, Adrienne Rich, and Sylvia Plath. Plath, the youngest, did not live past the dismantling.

And here, now, is what people in the social sciences call a control group. In 1976 Philip Appleman, noticing how many poets as well as himself would turn fifty that year, wrote a delightful pastiche or multiple parody he called "A Questionnaire to the Poets of 1926." He answered the "questionnaire" as each of his fellow poets born in 1926 might have answered it; there are eleven of them, including W. D. Snodgrass, who was to have a great effect on Sexton and Kumin. (Robert Lowell and Theodore Roethke, were, alas, born too soon for Appleman's poetic purposes on that occasion: chronology is rarely tidy.) His covering poem began: "Born in the year / Rilke died, you are all / creeping up on death . . ." And the "Snodgrass" poem starts: "So what did you expect, / To get younger every year? / As everything else went sere / and yellow, we'd resurrect?"

But that's exactly what the women of that generation did: resurrect, move toward rebirth and beyond. Appleman's poets commented on the world, a mess, and the loss of youth, a sorrow, but they neither dismantled the past nor considered restructing the future. In contrast to the men in Appleman's poem, this remarkable generation of women poets is a watershed. They found a frankly autobiographical, "confessional" mode for their poetry and discovered a form for their uninhibited autobiographical impulses. These clearly outspoken autobiographical efforts offer details of personal rebellion and sudden, dazzling recognition of too easily accepted female servitude with a forthrightness that would have been unthinkable two decades earlier. It is, one might add, happily ironic that women poets like Sylvia Plath and Anne Sexton were given

"permission" for their new frankness about their personal lives
by the confessional poetry of male poets W. D. Snodgrass and
Robert Lowell. Encouraged originally by that example, women
began to seize upon their own stories, and to tell them with a
directness that shocks as it enlightens. It certainly shocked
James Dickey, who, reviewing poetry by Anne Sexton in the
New York Times Book Review in 1963, wrote: "It would be
hard to find a writer who dwells more insistently on the pa-
thetic and disgusting aspects of bodily experience, as though
this made the writing more real, and it would also be difficult
to find a more hopelessly mechanical approach to reporting
these matters than the one she employs" (quoted in Sexton,
166).

   In recent years, two collections of autobiographical essays
by women have been published—*Fathers: Reflections by
Daughters,* edited by Ursula Owen, and *Between Women:
Biographers, Novelists, Critics, Teachers and Artists Write
About Their Work on Women,* edited by Carol Ascher, Louise
DeSalvo, and Sara Ruddick—which exemplify how far women
have come in their perceptions of, among much else, the role
of parents in their lives. Following in the path opened by the
women poets of "my" generation, the writers in these collections examine with new awareness the hitherto mutely accepted constraints on their lives. Their parents and other male
and female figures are seen with sharp distinctions. One can
generalize from these essays with minor, if any, exaggeration
that fathers, as representatives of the patriarchy, are the pivot
on which, usually in memory, the new awareness turns. Mothers have no obvious role in this change, but some other female
mentor or figure, often not even known personally, most often
dead, operates in the new female plot to enhance the reaction
from the father and encourage or inspire the awakening. Mothers may come to be recognized with a new, loving perception,

but it is not mothers who free women from their fathers. They leave their daughters as yet unawakened.

Fathers have so clearly represented the patriarchy to newly awakened feminists that in 1983 Sheila Rowbotham felt the need to defend the individuality of fathers: "Because we were not dealing with abstractions of a vaguely defined 'patriarchy' but talking about actual men, a complex picture began to emerge of 'manhood' and 'fatherhood' and our contradictory needs and images of both. Because these were men with whom we were connected passionately and intimately, however painfully, it was impossible to settle for an oversimplified stereotype in which they could be objectified as 'the enemy' or even 'the other' " (quoted in Owen, 213). Such a statement, amounting to forgiveness of the father, or at least an understanding of him, which almost all women autobiographers seem eventually to reach, must not be allowed to obscure the great difficulty women have in coming to terms with this figure. As Maxine Kumin has said, the poem about her father was "the hardest poem I ever wrote." She wrote it originally in syllabics and rhyme, using these as a defense between her and the material of the poem: "That's how terrified I was of writing it" (1979b, 27).

This terror of analyzing one's relation to the father, as Kumin describes it, in no way denies that, until recently, confronting the relation to the father was the only way to female self-realization. As Adrienne Rich has observed: "It is a painful fact that a nurturing father, who replaces rather than complements a mother, *must be loved at the mother's expense*, whatever the reasons for the mother's absence" (1976, 245). The essays in *Between Women* demonstrate further that when a woman sought a female model for self-realization and achievement, she had to find it in a woman who had died (this is true of almost all the essays in the book), and she was enabled to find it, as the ages of the contributors testify, only with the encouragement of the current feminist movement. Without these dead women, and without the feminist current bearing the lonely female swimmer along, the discovery and use of a female model would have been impossible. Maxine Kumin writes: "I began as a poet in the Dark Ages of the fifties with very little sense of who I was—a wife, a daughter, a mother, a college instructor, a swimmer, a horse lover, a hermit—a stewpot of conflicting emotions" (1979b, 106).

Adrienne Rich, whose autobiography is to be found not in a single book but rather in her poems and in diverse parts of her prose works, has nevertheless done more than anyone else to revolutionize women's autobiography. Rich records how she sought again and again to identify herself in new ways, ways guaranteed to be upsetting to the neat, orderly world from which she came. Her most fundamental struggle was to recognize herself as a poet, and to mean by this that the quality of what she felt impelled to say in poetry was not diminished because it was thought to be female, political, and offensive. Rich, like all of her class and generation, grew up with anthologies of poetry we were convinced represented a "universal vision." "I still believed that poets were inspired by some transcendent authority and spoke from some extraordinary height." Although she had been born a woman, she "was trying to think and act as if poetry—and the possibility of making poems— were a truly universal—that is, gender-neutral—realm. In the universe of masculine paradigm, I naturally absorbed ideas about women, sexuality, power, from the subjectivity of male poets." Of course she was told that her sort of poetry, "that is, writing from a perspective which may not be male, or white, or heterosexual, or middle-class," was grinding a political ax, that what she was writing was "bitter" and "personal' (1986a, 175, 179, 180).

Rich has written, in both poems and essays, of many women

who preceded her, from Emily Dickinson to the Russian women's climbing team that perished. But, while in the creation of her autobiography Rich writes with loving attention of her female predecessors, it is her father with whom she has had to come to terms; it is her father who is the pivot upon which her autobiography ultimately turns. And, like Woolf, she is over fifty when she finally comes to terms with him in print, and identifies herself: she knows that in the rest of her life, "every aspect of her identity will have to be engaged. The middle-class white girl taught to trade obedience for privilege. The Jewish lesbian raised to be a heterosexual gentile. The woman who first heard oppression named and analyzed in the Black civil rights struggle. The woman with three sons, the feminist who hates male violence. The woman limping with a cane, the woman who has stopped bleeding, are also accountable. The poet who knows that beautiful language can lie, that the oppressor's language sometimes sounds beautiful" (1986a, 123). One can scarcely imagine a woman so identifying herself in print two decades ago: it is Rich who best demonstrates the new autobiographical form which permitted, indeed demanded, that such a statement be openly made.

Rich began her prose writings in the autobiographical mode in her profoundly important and shocking book, *Of Woman Born*. Her honesty in this book, her admission that women might at times hate their children, might even have murderous thoughts about them, so shocked the women who were its first reviewers that the book was denied much of the publicity and exposure that had, before the reviews, been offered. Rich wrote at the beginning of that work: "It seemed to me impossible from the first to write a book of this kind without being often autobiographical, without often saying 'I.' Yet for many months I buried my head in historical research and analysis in order to delay or prepare the way for the plunge into areas of my own

life which were painful and problematical" (1976, 15–16). Rich
asserted here, as she had previously, her belief that it is only
the willingness of women to share their "private and often
painful experience" that will enable them to achieve a true
description of the world, and to free and encourage one another. Feminist theoreticians like Elaine Showalter have, since
then, defended this female mode, despite efforts to dismiss it
by calling it confessional. "In comparison to this flowing confessional criticism," she wrote, "the tight-lipped Olympian intelligence" of writers such as Elizabeth Hardwick and Susan Sontag
"can seem arid and strained" (1982, 19). They can also seem
self-protective, and too readily conforming to the male model
of distance and apparent disinterest.

In *Of Woman Born,* Rich spoke many hidden truths. That
only when visibly pregnant did she feel, in her whole adult
life, not-guilty. That, like so many women with "male" dreams
in childhood, she had set her heart on a son, and had felt
triumphant over her mother, who had brought forth only
daughters, at the birth of her "perfect, golden, male child."
That her husband's "helping" was unusual in the 1950s, but
there was no question that the major career was his, all the
initiative for domestic responsibilities hers. She reports what
she wrote in her journal in those years, the despair, resolu-
tions, self-hatred, anger, weariness, bouts of weeping characteristic of so many women's journals. Nor was she willing to
dismiss her despair during her children's early years as "the
human condition." As she noted, "those who speak largely of
the human condition are usually those most exempt from its
oppressions—whether of sex, race, or servitude."

By then (1976), Rich's poetry had already broken through
the barriers of impersonality and the lack of tolerance for autobiography in women's poetry. Contemporary male poets,
principally Robert Lowell and W. D. Snodgrass, had chosen

the same path. But it is chiefly in Rich's generation of women poets—Plath, Sexton, Kumin, Kizer, Cooper, Levertov—that T. S. Eliot's ban upon the personal was defied. These same women—certainly Plath, Sexton, and Kumin—began, like Rich, to explore in other genres their previously hidden resentments and experiences, guilts and sufferings. Novels, interviews, letters all served this impulse. But it is Rich alone who, in writing an essay devoted to her father, practiced the new female autobiography directly, in prose.

The writing of this essay, "Split at the Root," seemed to her "so dangerous an act, filled with fear and shame," but nonetheless necessary. It is well to take these words at their face value. If women's autobiography has made a great leap, it has not done so without great pain and courage on the part of women like Rich. What became central to Rich's account of her father was not only what had been denied her as a woman but what had been denied her as a Jew. Her father's devoted belief in "passing," in making it into the gentile world by being so like gentiles that they would forgive him his Jewishness, is what she chiefly remembers and resents about him: "With enough excellence, you could presumably make it stop mattering that you were Jewish; you could become the *only* Jew in the gentile world. . . . I had never been taught about resistance, only about passing." And to pass meant to be the right sort of Jew, one who exemplified "achievement, aspiration, genius, idealism. Whatever was unacceptable got left back, under the rubric of Jewishness, or the 'wrong kind' of Jews: uneducated, aggressive, loud" (1986a, 110, 107).

To disconnect herself from her family, Rich married a "real Jew." Perhaps she was simultaneously rejecting her Protestant mother and attempting to transform, to humanize, her father. There may also be an indirect connection, for Rich suggests that the efforts of fathers to be accepted in the male world they do not question or challenge are vitally connected with their efforts to imprison their female children, however talented and encouraged, in the conventions of femininity.

Anne Sexton once explained to an interviewer:

Until I was twenty-eight I had a kind of buried self who didn't know she could do anything but make white sauce and diaper babies. I didn't know I had any creative depths. I was a victim of the American Dream, the bourgeois, middle class dream. All I wanted was a little piece of life, to be married, to have children. I thought the nightmares, the visions, the demons would go away if there was enough love to put them down. I was trying my damndest to lead a conventional life, for that was how I was brought up, and it was what my husband wanted of me. But one can't build little white picket fences to keep nightmares out. The surface cracked when I was about twenty-eight. I had a psychotic breakdown and tried to kill myself. [1977, 399–400]

The importance of this passage lies in its truth, which women could not tell before. But there are two other points that Diane Middlebrook has clearly identified for us: that "Sexton experienced the home as a sphere of confinement and stultification," and that she escaped through the way of death (25). For Sexton and Plath, suicide became a part of life, so violent was the action necessary for rebirth and truth. As Carolyn Kizer puts it: "From Sappho to myself, consider the fate of women. / How unwomanly to discuss it!"

"White men have politely debated free will," she writes. "We have howled for it." But we have still been, as Kizer knows, "custodians of the world's best-kept secret: / Merely the private lives of one-half of humanity" (from "Pro Femina").

Until two decades ago, it was the world's best-kept secret, and women were its best custodians, speaking for men. Louise Bogan, in the early 1920s: "Women have no wilderness in them, / They are provident instead, / Content in the tight hot cell of their hearts, To eat dusty bread." Until Sexton, Kumin, Rich, Plath, and the others burst from their tight hot cell, to invent a new form—woman's truth—she was right. Diane Middlebrook has said of Sexton's "rapid and improbable" success that, "like that of most writers, [it] resulted from a combination of talent, hard work and well-timed good luck."

The times helped. Women found the courage to demand what millennia had told them it was not reasonable to demand. As Kumin wrote: "I am tired of this history of loss / What drum can I beat to reach you? / To be reasonable / Is to put out the light. / To be reasonable is to let go" (from "September 22").

Jane McCabe tells us: "Through anger, the truth looks simple." We all know the truth of that. It appears, therefore, that women had not, until the 1960s, enough anger to see a simple truth, which must always precede complex truths. Plath saw it in the last year of her life; poems overtook her like a revelation. For the first time, it would seem, in the poets of that generation, there was an anger they could tap into, an anger they could not turn in upon themselves. Kumin and Rich, both Jewish, connect that anger with Jewishness, with the failure to recognize, in Hannah Arendt's words, that "if we do not know our own history, we are doomed to live it as though it were our private fate." Arendt never applied that lesson to women; she was content to be an exceptional woman "in the tight, hard cell of her heart." The group of poets I here celebrate learned, however, that they were living history as private fate, a lesson those who were Jews may have learned with particular pungency. Remember that Plath, who was not Jewish, saw herself, symbolically, as a Jew, not to claim suffering she had not earned, as Irving Howe thought, but precisely to recognize her suffering as connected—much as Woolf had told us a few years before her death—to fascism.

In the old style "autobiography," women never told of their love for other women. That love is various, wide enough to include all women, narrow enough to focus, for a lifetime or the life of a passion, on one other woman. It is this love, I am certain, this sense of identification with women alone, not as fellow sufferers but as fellow achievers and fighters in the public domain, upon which the success of the current feminist movement depends. Some of the poets we have been discussing moved in and out of marriages (Sexton, Rich, Plath, Kizer); or they stayed within a marriage and remade it (Kumin); or they never married (Cooper); or they discovered the love of women and the terrors of compulsory heterosexuality (Rich); or they found friendships (Kumin and Sexton). But above all, they thought of women as "we." They loved and respected one another, sharing and admitting one another to their fates. They learned that women cannot be alone, identified only with the men at hand. They learned that wherever they are, even in the White House (or No. 10 Downing Street), there must be other women with them as peers. Sexton and her friend Lois Ames wore gold disks on which they had had engraved: "Don't let the bastards win." They agreed to proclaim that together.

It was the task of this generation more to dismantle the past than to imagine the future. But Rich has never stopped trying to imagine it. "I think," she wrote, "women have a mission to survive . . . and to be whole people. I believe that this can save the world, but I don't think that women have a mission to clean up after men's messes. I think we have to save the world by doing it for ourselves—for all women—I don't mean some narrow, restricted notion of who women are, only white women or only middle-class women and only Western women" (quoted in Martin, 232).

Some years ago she wrote of "the leap we talked of taking," a leap that "my generation" took. But in the times that fol-

lowed, Rich recognized, she had lived that leap, "not as a leap /
 but a succession of brief, amazing moments / each one making
possible the next." And in a later poem called "What Is Possible," she understands that the philosophical language we have
 inherited will not enable us to describe the future, or even to
wish for what such a vision might foresee:

> If the mind were clear
> and if the mind were simple   you could take this mind
> this particular state   and say
> *This is how I would live if I could choose:*
> *this is what is possible . . .*
>   But the mind
> of the woman imagining all this   the mind
> that allows all this to be possible . . .
> does not so easily
>   work free from remorse
> does not so easily
>   manage the miracle
> for which mind is famous
>   or used to be famous
> does not at will become abstract and pure
> this woman's mind
> does not even will that miracle
> having a different mission
>   in the universe.

In 1972, Anne Sexton inscribed a copy of *The Book of Folly*
for her friend Maxine Kumin: "Dear Max—from now on, it's
our world." Women would not have said that to one another
before.

I have defined "my" generation rigidly, extending it only
to include Plath, the youngest poet I've discussed, for whom
nonetheless World War II was a source of profound metaphor.
Had I chosen an earlier date, I might have encompassed other

important women poets: Elizabeth Bishop, Gwendolyn Brooks, May Sarton, Louise Bogan, Muriel Ruykeyser. I see a profound break in the poets of the generation I chose to define. Less defensible is my ending with Plath when, by reaching two years later, I might have included Audre Lorde (born in 1934). If Audre Lorde does not belong with the World War II generation, it is because she, her life, and her work have focused on other patterns and influences: the work of black writers not available, because of chronology or the narrowness of canons, to white women;* the influence on her of African writers and narratives; and her leap to outspokenness by which she appears, compared to the women of my generation, to have claimed identity sooner and more sharply, without the same struggle. She announced that she was a "black lesbian feminist warrior poet." Her struggle to become herself was different from the struggle of white middle-class women. She found African goddesses more empowering, perhaps, than a white woman poet would find goddesses from Greece or Christianity, though black women writers have written of these also:

> I speak without concern for the accusations
> that I am too much or too little woman
> that I am too black or too white
> or too much myself
> and through my lips come the voices
> of the ghosts of our ancestors
> living and moving among us

and also,

---

* And perhaps even to black; Alice Walker reports that it was only in college that she first heard of Zora Neale Hurston, and then only her name. In a course on black writers she took at Jackson State College in Mississippi, black women writers "were names appended, live verbal footnotes, to the illustrious all-male list that parallelled them" [84].

I
is the total black, being spoken
from the earth's inside.
There are many kinds of open
how a diamond comes into a knot of flame
how sound comes into a word, colored
by who pays what for speaking.

. . . .

Love is a word, another kind of open.
As the diamond comes into a knot of flame
I am Black because I come from the earth's inside
now take my word for jewel in the open light.

By the time of *The Cancer Journal*, Lorde, writing of illness, woman as victim and survivor, and the sole saving grace
of female friendship, speaks, across race, national, or class
boundaries, for what is now *her* generation of women. Female
friendship has been given its first and most compelling text by
black women writers of this generation. Toni Morrison has
said: "Friendship between women is special, different, and has
never been depicted as the major focus of a novel before *Sula*"
(118). It had not been depicted in an autobiographical work as
a major focus of a woman's life before the work of Audre Lorde
and her generation.

Four

---

*Female, a Quixote is no Quixote at all; told
about a woman, the tale of being caught in a fantasy
becomes the story of everyday life.*

—RACHEL BROWNSTEIN

ISS [Mary Russell] MITFORD SAID, when asked
if she would not have liked to have been married, "No, I never wanted a full, normal life."
This happy denial of the joys of the married
state was invoked by Ivy Compton-Burnett and her lifelong
companion, Margaret Jourdain, in explanation of their refusal
to marry. Hilary Spurling, quoting them, went on to observe
that "middle age suited them both. They had arrived together
(and for the first time in each case) at an orderly and highly
agreeable existence designed to please nobody but themselves" (161).

The "themselves" in this sentence must be noted. For the
most part, marriage has suited the man, and appeared to suit
the woman because she was satisfied with the rewards offered
in place of her own self-determination. The fact of their middle
age must also be noted. One sign of a marriage that has invented itself, that is to say, has become sufficiently flexible to
allow autonomy in both its partners, appears in middle age
when the obvious sexual attractions of the woman are dimin-

ished, or gone, and when the man feels toward her not just
loyalty and tolerance but joy and anticipation. The woman in
middle age who has married a man she respects but does not
love in the sense of being lost in passion can say, with Virginia
Woolf at nearly sixty, "and my heart stood still with pride that
he had ever married me." Such men and women have reinvented marriage.

Marriage is the most persistent of myths imprisoning women,
and misleading those who write of women's lives. Angela Carter
has written: "All the mythic versions of women, from the myth
of the redeeming purity of the virgin to that of the healing,
reconciling mother, are consolatory nonsenses; and consolatory nonsense seems to me a fair definition of myth, anyway"
(5). Carter does not mention marriage here, yet both virginity
and motherhood define the married woman, enclose her. Marriage without children at its center, understood as a system of
mutual support has largely been beyond the imaginative reach
of either biographers or living women.

There have always been women who chose not to marry,
or who wished for the chance so to choose. One of the most
persistent misconceptions about single women is that they do
not marry because they cannot find a man, or because they
have not been able to entice one they have found into matrimony. An article in the *New York Times* on December 13,
1986, entitled "Why Few American Women Marry," reflects
this misconception. The authors, who had previously published a report on American marriage patterns, mentioned that
their study was reported under headlines like: "Single-Minded
College Girls Put on Shelf at 30," "No M.R.S. Degree for
Those Who Wait," "Women Who Tarry May Never Marry,"
and so forth. Complaining about this hype, Neil Bennet and
David Bloom observed that the major issue reflected in their
statistics is that "a woman's status no longer derives primarily

from the man to whom she is married." They discussed the redefinition of roles which lies at the heart of their findings: "One out of every eight women born in the mid-1950s will never marry, compared to one in 25 women in the preceding generation. Nearly one of five college-educated white women born in the 1950's will never marry. Among young black women, whether college-educated or not, almost three in ten will never marry. Simply put, the extent to which young women today are not marrying is making demographic and social history."

Some of this downturn in marriage, they remark, is doubtless involuntary. "But there has also been a voluntary shift in marriage patterns resulting from women's greater economic and social independence and their liberation from the assumption of motherhood. Unfortunately, this positive side of the study has had a difficult time finding its way into print. Rather, the press's depiction of a spinster boom on the horizon sent an ear-splitting alarm. . . . Women who had postponed marriage were frightened into believing marriage for them was now impossible, while other women were criticized for their 'selfishness' and accused of undermining America's perhaps most cherished institution, the family."

In her biography of Vanessa Bell (Virginia Woolf's sister), Frances Spalding writes: "Whereas Virginia Woolf enjoyed the security of a respectable marriage . . . Vanessa lived most of her life in a relationship not recognized by church or state, with the man by whom she had an illegitimate daughter." Spalding therefore calls Vanessa "far more revolutionary" (xv). Yet Spalding herself records Vanessa Bell's devotion to Duncan Grant, so extreme that she welcomed his young male lovers in her house. Clearly, Spalding finds revolutionary something that *is* marriage but dares not speak its name.

What is truly revolutionary in marriage? Can anything be, if the ancient dyad of man and woman is in place? What might

biographers look for that has, so far, been insufficiently noticed? In the case of Ivy Compton-Burnett and Margaret Jourdain we seem to have a pattern, but they are two women. Can
two women give us a pattern for marriage?

After Gertrude Stein published *The Autobiography of
Alice B. Toklas* in 1933, my mother regarded Stein's life as
emblematic of freedom. Both when I was a teenager and later,
after the war, she and I read and discussed books by people
who had known Stein, some of them American soldiers Stein
had befriended, and in my mother's eyes the life Stein and
Toklas shared broke free of the shackles of ordinary female
existence. We did not, of course, recognize them as lesbians;
I'm not sure I even knew the word. And when my husband
suggested this fact, I snorted: obviously, they didn't do "that,"
whatever "that" was.

Wiser now, I still find something essentially heterosexual
and conventional in the relationship of Stein and Toklas, despite my mature awareness of their lesbian relationship. Students have argued with me vociferously on this point. Yet, as
Jane Rule points out in *Lesbian Images,* Gertrude Stein "per-
suaded Alice to accept a relationship as nearly patterned on a
middle-class marriage as possible, in which Gertrude would
be the husband, Alice the wife, all understanding, tending,
admiring. But Alice, though she absolutely accepted Gertrude
Stein's importance, was obviously not in awe of her. . . . She
seems to have managed Gertrude much as any other loving
and clever wife has managed a husband who needs to feel
superior but is bound by dependent needs, both emotional
and practical." Gertrude would, Rule observes, "change any
decision if confronted by Alice's tears" (71). Without Alice, we
now understand, Gertrude could not write. Theirs was, nonetheless, a relationship we see duplicated in the lives of many
male writers and their devoted wives, who combine muse,

nurturer, and general factotum in one body.

Alice typed, and cooked, and gardened, and corrected, and talked to wives. She joined the Catholic Church after Stein's death. Catharine Stimpson has noted that "as Stein had been her husband, she now found solace and happiness in priests and patriarchal structures" (134). "Probably," Stimpson continues, "Stein and Toklas would have been less celebrated, and thought more dangerous, if they had been more overtly equalitarian, if Toklas had stood less often in the background of their portrait." Stein and Toklas certainly "announced the value of a woman's we-ness" (135). But, as I can testify, we thought in those conventional times that Stein had been clever enough to get herself a wife, without, of course, meaning. . . . We did, I think, perceive that there was in that "woman's we-ness" a chance for tenderness and laughter beyond the range of the man-woman relationship; we spoke of this, however, wholly in terms of freedom to do what one wanted. It was Stein whom my mother envied, not Toklas.

In 1942, David Daiches commented on the marriage of Virginia and Leonard Woolf in words no one then thought to quarrel with:

She was fortunate in her marriage. Her husband, Leonard Woolf, journalist, publicist, political thinker and general essayist, was a man of lively and sympathetic mind, keenly interested in literature and indeed in almost everything and sufficiently aware of his wife's talent to encourage her from the first in her career as a writer. . . . In the course of a distinguished career he was to display his versatile talents in many fields, his writings ranging from a bitter analysis of Britain's policy towards the black races in Africa to fiction. . . . The marriage of a woman of genius to a man of great talent ought by all the laws to have ended in a mess. [5–6]

What are all the laws? They are those that allow the experience of questing—the right, as Stimpson puts it, to "plumb language and define culture" (131)—only to men and a very few exceptional women like Stein. (Exceptional women are the chief imprisoners of nonexceptional women, simultaneously proving that any woman could do it and assuring, in their uniqueness among men, that no other woman will.) Despite all the criticism that Woolf scholars in America have leveled against Leonard, and the scorn that Woolf critics in England have leveled against them both for their social position and class, these two had a revolutionary marriage, which I would define simply as one in which both partners have work at the center of their lives and must find a delicate balance that can support both together and each individually. This means of course that the man, or the exceptional woman in an all-woman relationship, must be equally, probably more, nurturing and supportive than the usual "husband." The marriage of a woman and man of talent must constantly be reinvented: its failure has already been predicted by conventional society, and its success is usually (Daiches being an exception here) disbelieved or denied.

Virginia Woolf, like Beatrice Webb, married a man who could, socially, be considered her inferior. As Gayle Rubin has shown in her historic essay, "The Traffic in Women," women are expected to marry "up": to marry men who are taller, richer, older, stronger, with at least the promise of more social clout. Thus is added to the privilege of gender all other privileges and powers. Woolf's husband was from a lower class than she, though not much lower, and he was a Jew. Webb's husband was definitely from a lower class, and a socialist. Neither woman found her potential husband physically compelling. Both men became devoted husbands and nurturers, one a successful lover, the other not. What marked both marriages was equality, in work and money; if there was a nurturer, a keeper-at-bay of social nuisances, it was the husband.

These marriages, like those of George Eliot and Elizabeth Barrett Browning (but unlike that of Jane Carlyle), are more meaningful to biographers than those of present-day women who may decline marriage altogether, or enjoy dual-career marriages, because the greater number of biographical subjects lived at a time when marriage appeared both conventional and mandatory. That certain women achieved this sort of marriage gives us clues as to what we must look for in the domestic relationships of women in the past. Above all, biographers must ignore both the Victorian, Freudian, Angel-in-the-House model of marriage and the woman's conviction that not to marry is to fail. (We have seen in chapter 2 how James Brabazon interpreted Dorothy Sayers in this light; a similar example is the opening of Martha Saxton's biography of Louisa May Alcott.) A young woman who is the child of a miserable marriage will respond in one of two ways: either she will assure herself that *her* marriage will be different, a hope that is fulfilled about as often as the bank is broken at Monte Carlo; or she will avoid marriage, or conventionally acceptable marriage, altogether.

If we divide the world into roles exclusively paternal or maternal (as, before Freud but even more frantically since, we seem destined to do), marriage will never reinvent itself. As Nancy Chodorow has demonstrated, the "family romance," in reinforcing itself generation upon generation, in fact makes itself unworkable: the boys and girls are not raised to relate productively to one another; the boy defines himself as "not woman," the girl does not learn sufficient individuation. In the rare cases, as with the Webbs and the Woolfs, where the husband has assumed what may be called a nurturing or maternal role, the man, even if he has originally been attracted to the woman by her beauty, will continue to love her, will allow her to exist outside of the "male gaze." He will judge her in their continuing marriage not as a reified object but as herself a subject, looking as he looks, measuring as he measures. But can a man love like a mother? Not, Nancy Miller observes, "if he positions himself in the line of the patriarchal gaze, which surveys, judges, regulates; not if he also occupies the place of the father; not if she also wants him *as a man* to love her *as a woman*" (186–87).

Miller goes on to quote Colette in describing what tempts a woman in a heterosexual couple: to live in the presence of "the eager spectator to one's life." But he must believe not only what he can see, what appears to his "male gaze," and the gaze, therefore, of other judging men, but what he sees of her life as a whole, including work, intelligence, talent, doubt, and achievement (187).

Colette more and more appears before us, in her life and her writings, as the paradigm of female autonomy, allowing us to glimpse a way toward treasured solitude and the vitality of an open life. Born into one destiny, she achieved, in later years, another. She had to flee an idyllic childhood, threatened by a maternal love so marvelous that the child had to shatter that life to avoid engulfment by the very natural and maternal beauty—which would, in retrospect, become her inspiration. Dowerless, Colette allowed herself to be married off to a man very much older than she, a profligate and pimp of other people's talents. She had never dreamed of being a writer, had never consciously thought of it; her biographer is struck by "the exceptional process by which [Colette] was brought to write," and "the time required before she achieved recognition as a writer" (Sarde 16). The exceptional process was that of being forced by her husband to write books about her girlhood experiences (the Claudine books) which were published under his name. Colette was fifty when she first published a novel under her own name, the single name she had chosen for herself. Meanwhile, she had married twice, had appeared in music halls and on the stage, had been a journalist, had had both male and female lovers, and had given birth to a child.

Sarde writes of Colette at fifty: "Man had finally been shorn of his magical and commanding force; he so longer either barred doors or opened them. For Colette, the days of compromise and sharing were over" (360). Colette found that renunciation was always part of the "lovely present"; Sarde sees this embodied in Lea in *The Last of Cheri,* who resembles Colette in her "penchant for renunciation for the sake of freedom," in her "abstentation" (351). What is renounced is the old way of love, being the object of male desire and the male gaze, that acknowledgment of personhood that, in the conventional world, only a man can bestow.

Colette did marry, late in life, a man much younger than she, who devoted his life to her until her death. Perhaps her fame, her power, her control of her life brought her this kind of devotion, more often seen when a woman's appeal is her money, which passes into her husband's control after her marriage. Colette, again, married "down": a younger, poorer, not famous man, who was a Jew. At her death she was the first woman in France to be accorded a state funeral.

Is it possible to redefine marriage, or is that institution already so close to extinction that we need not try? Women have legally transformed the marriage relation in under 150 years: we must ask whether that transformation is not in itself amazing, or whether, on the other hand, it has not, as transformations go, been laggardly.

In 1854, Barbara Leigh Smith Bodichon published a pamphlet, "Married Women and the Law"; the following excerpt reminds us exactly where women were almost 150 years ago.

A man and wife are one person in law; the wife loses all her rights as a single woman, and her existence is entirely absorbed in that of her husband. He is civilly responsible for her acts; she lives under his protection or cover, and her condition is called coverture.

A woman's body belongs to her husband; she is in his custody, and he can enforce his right by a writ of *habeas corpus*.

What was her personal property before marriage, such as money in hand, money at the bank, jewels, household goods, clothes, etc., becomes absolutely her husband's, and he may assign or dispose of them at his pleasure whether he and his wife live together or not.

A wife's *chattels real* (i.e., estates) become her husband's.

Neither the Courts of Common law nor Equity have any direct power to oblige a man to support his wife. . . .

The legal custody of children belongs to the father. During the life-time of a sane father, the mother has no rights over her children, except a limited power over infants, and the father may take them from her and dispose of them as he thinks fit.

A married woman cannot sue or be sued for contracts—nor can she enter into contracts except as the agent of her husband; that is to say, her word alone is not binding in law. . . .

A wife cannot bring actions unless the husband's name is joined.

A husband and wife cannot be found guilty of conspiracy, as that offence cannot be committed unless there are two persons.

In the last years of the twentieth century, it is unclear whether women who refer to themselves as, for example, Mrs. Thomas Smith know what servitude they are representing in that nomenclature. The same might be said today of women who exchange their last name for their husband's. Particularly with the statistical chances of a marriage ending, it is confusing for women not to keep the same name throughout their lives. Any possible ambivalence about this matter should surely have ended by the beginning of the 1980s at the latest.

Beside the Bodichon record of a married woman's nonpersonhood, it is instructive to place an account written a century later of a common stage presentation—partnering in ballet—as transformed by George Balanchine, however unintentionally, into a metaphor for marriage:

New York City Ballet is the company where partners scarcely touch. One of the unique aspects of the company is a special approach to partnering, the art of the man's presenting the woman and supporting her in her lifts, extended arabesques and multiple turns. While on the surface New York City Ballet's practices resemble those of other schools of ballet, a careful examination of the technique of partnering here reveals that the dancers have transformed the mechanics of support into something original and surprising.

Conventionally, the role of the partner is to supplement the ballerina's strength, to create the illusion that she can balance longer, soar higher, spin more quickly and securely. George Balanchine took the situation and transformed it. He wanted the ballerina to possess, genuinely, on her own, the strengths and abilities partnering had created the illusion she commanded. Today at NYCB, the woman acknowledges her partner out of generosity of spirit and a desire to share the challenge of dancing, but she does not really rely on him. . . . There is no missing the companywide distinguishing feature of minimal support. . . . The pas de deux should give the woman maximum freedom, liberty rather than dependence. . . . Perhaps most important are promenades, moments when the woman, balanced in arabesque, attitude or passe, is displayed from all angles as her partner walks around her. As he does so, and it is remarkable, he supports her, if possible, not with his hand, but with the merest touch of his fingertips on hers. [Finkel 4–5, 34]

It is noteworthy that few works of fiction make marriage their central concern. As Northrup Frye puts it, with his accustomed clarity: "The heroine who becomes a bride, and eventually, one assumes, a mother, on the last page of a romance, has accommodated herself to the cyclical movement: by her marriage . . . she completes the cycle and passes out of the story. We are usually given to understand that a happy and well-adjusted sexual life does not concern us as readers" (80). Fiction has largely rejected marriage as a subject, except in those instances where it is presented as a history of betrayal—at worst an Updike hell, at best what Auden speaks of as a game calling for "patience, foresight, maneuver, like war, like marriage." Marriage is very different than fiction presents it as being. We rarely examine its unromantic aspects. The romance was necessary not only to give form to male adventures and female lives but to maintain marriage itself. For if marriage is seen without its romantic aspects, it ceases to be attractive to its female half and, hence, is no longer useful to its patriarchal supporters.

In Shaw's 1908 play *Getting Married*, a bride-to-be reads the marriage service, is shocked, and almost refuses to go through with the ceremony. Robert Graves reports in *Goodbye to All That* that in 1918, when he married a young woman who had been kept in a continuous state of anger by the attitude of the Huntingdon men to their wives and daughters, nature followed art: "Nancy had read the marriage service for the first time that morning, and been so disgusted that she all but refused to go through with the wedding, though I had arranged for the ceremony to be modified and reduced to the shortest possible form" (272). Isadora Duncan, at least in the movie version of her life (in which she was portrayed by Vanessa Redgrave), expresses the view that any woman who has read the marriage service and marries deserves what she gets. Yet women, laughing at such lines, have chosen not to heed the ramifications of marriage, apparently fearing any interference with the sanctioned fulfillment of romance.

For women, the only sane way to live through a romance is to live through it without closure. Marriage to a lover is fatal; lovers are not husbands. More important, husbands are not lovers. The compulsion to find a lover and husband in a single person has doomed more women to misery than any other illusion. "A love affair brings human beings unnaturally together," John Bayley has written, "while marriage keeps them the right dignified distance apart" (229). But love, with its temporary togetherness, does not prepare a woman for the narrow life that lies for her on the other side of that "dignified distance."

The illusion that lovers can be husbands is carefully fostered by the patriarchy it serves. That is why Tolstoy isolates Anna Karenina, punishing her for daring to live with a lover outside the bonds of marriage. He wrote in his diary: "Anna is deprived of all these joys of occupying herself with the woman's side of life, because she is alone. All women have turned away from her, and she has nobody to talk to about all that which composes the everyday, purely feminine occupations" (Tolstoy 751). Furthermore, as Stern has observed, "many of the things she does—she rides in a man's habit, smokes, plays tennis, practices birth control, takes morphine against insomnia , keeps a disreputable English nurse, discusses Zola and Daudet—he strongly disapproves of" (Stern 863). Women who chose to live with a lover were long condemned to such isolation; married women, powerless in their marriages, joined with the patriarchy in isolating those who dared to live out other plots. Was marriage always in such danger of becoming unappealing to women that the whole society had to contrive to keep the fiction of its desirability alive and intact?

Today women can choose not to marry and can live with lovers before marriage or throughout their lives, serially or otherwise. Today women can refuse to see marriage as their destiny, as men have always refused to see it. Some, like Oriana Fallaci, choose against marriage because "marriage is an expression that to me suggests 'giving up,' an expression of sacrifice and regret. . . . The solitude [I needed] wasn't a physical solitude. . . . It was an internal solitude that comes about from the fact of being a woman—and a woman with responsibilities in the world of men. . . . Today, I need that kind of solitude so much—since it is what moves me, intellectually speaking—that sometimes I feel the need to be physically alone.

When I'm with my companion, there are moments when we are two too many. I never get bored when I'm alone, and I get easily bored when I'm with others" (12).

Fallaci, unlike Anna Karenina, was not forced to accept isolation as the price of physical passion. The difference today is precisely that women no longer accept, either for themselves or for other women who live outside of matrimony, the isolation the patriarchy would like to impose. Yet, when all the dangers of matrimony have been perceived, there are women who choose to marry, know what they are doing, and decide that life with a man, with or without children, is what they desire. With rights now to their own property and earnings, with rights to their children, with rights to make contracts and to function as autonomous individuals in the world, they still choose to join with a man. It is for these women, and for the men who choose to love them and to stay with them, that new definitions and a new reality about marriage must be not only lived but narrated. "It is time that someone wrote a new plot," a character of Virginia Woolf's says in *Between the Acts.* Since that novel ends with a man and woman at the beginning of the world beginning again in a new play, Woolf may have meant that it was time someone wrote a new plot for marriage. She wrote one with her life, but never with her fiction; nor did George Eliot, or Beatrice Webb—nor has anyone.

All the same, Nigel Nicolson, who edited Woolf's letters and who, no feminist, has been placed in the odd position of reporting on his parents' unconventional marriage as well as that of the Woolfs, describes the marriage of Virginia and Leonard Woolf in ways fiction has not matched:

> When two people of independent minds marry, they must be able to rely upon each other's tolerance, affection and support. Each must encourage, without jealousy, the full development of the other's gifts, each allow the other privacy, different interests, different

friends. But they must share an intellectual and moral base. One of them cannot be philistine if the other is constantly breasting new ideas. They cannot disagree wildly on what is right and wrong. Above all, their love must grow as passion fades. . . . [Leonard and Virginia Woolf] never experienced jealousy of another person or of a talent unshared. She deeply respected his judgement on what meant most to her, her writing; and he, lacking the flight of soaring imagination and recognizing that she possessed it, shielded her, watched her fluctuating health, nurtured her genius, and with instinctive understanding left her alone in a room of her own, while he remained always available in the common room between them. [xiii, xiv]

The past years have seen harsh criticism of Leonard—some of it, given the complexities of human life, deserved. He was on a few occasions wrong in his judgments of her work. One cannot but feel that to go behind her back to doctors, to impose upon her a regimen she dreaded, was to decide too readily that he knew more about her needs than she knew or could understand. I even believe that Leonard, in failing to understand, as he seemed uniquely qualified to do, the connection between the subjection of women and the misuse of authority epitomized in fascism failed in an important intellectual way. But one knows even today sympathetic and supportive men who fail thus. It is not easy to forgive Leonard any of these things, and Woolf scholars, feminist and not, have been angrily critical of him. But it is well to remember that he was backed up in his decisions by all the medical knowledge of his day as well as by Virginia's sister, Vanessa, and that he was there coping, not advising from a safe distance, and without the benefit of hindsight. I believe that in failing to appreciate *this* marriage, even if it was not perfect, as few things human are, we go a certain way toward denying altogether the possibility of any good marriage. I concur with Quentin Bell, even less a feminist than Nicolson, that marrying Leonard was the wisest thing Virginia did. I believe that he made her writing life possible.

What it comes down to, perhaps, is how infrequently married couples are friends, and how often we consider friendship as being opposed to, or excluding, love. C. S. Lewis has asked, "Suppose you are fortunate enough to have 'fallen in love' and married your Friend. And now suppose it possible that you were offered the choice of two futures; '*Either* you two will cease to be lovers but remain forever joint seekers of the same God, the same beauty, the same truth, *or else*, losing all that, you will retain as long as you live the raptures and ardours, all the wonder and the wild desire of Eros. Choose which you please.' Which should we choose?" (64). It is of course obvious that Lewis sees friendship as the enduring choice and "the raptures and ardours" as inevitably temporary. But he is not capable—or at least was not when he wrote these lines—of believing in friendship between men and women, nor of passion enduring in that friendship. Since passion between men was forbidden, he, like Montaigne, seems to have had no earthly model for either friendship or marriage. By the end of his life, having loved and married late, Lewis might well have believed in it and described it as marriage. He may have discovered that passion and friendship are not mutually exclusive, and that passion is to be found not only with a lover in a state of ecstatic infatuation but with a wife or husband as well.

W. H. Auden, who never married (except officially to help Erica Mann escape from Nazi Germany), described it is a "healthy mixture of physical desire and *philia*, a mutual personal liking based on common interests and values," where "the dominant feeling is of mutual respect between equals" (64). It is easy enough to say that this is the definition of a man who was never there, although late in life he did ask Hannah Arendt to marry him. The truth is that marriage is difficult to imagine, and has been envisioned only by those who may not have had typical marriages, or any marriages at all, but who

understood friendship and used it as a model. Even for George
Eliot, who had just such a marriage as Auden described, the
creation of such a marriage in fiction was impossible. It is a
thought worth pondering.

Most of us begin, aided by almost every aspect of our culture, hoping for a perfect marriage. What this means is that we
accept sexual attractiveness as a clue to finding our way in the
labyrinth of marriage. It almost never is. Oddly enough, the
media, which promise marriage as the happy ending, almost
simultaneously show it, after several years, to be more ending
than happy. But the dream lives on that this time will be different.

Perhaps the reason the truth is so little told is that it sounds
quotidian, bourgeois, even like advocating proportion, that
most unappealing of all virtues. But E. M. Forster understood
this: when someone suggested that truth is halfway between
extremes, his answer (in *Howards End*) was, "No; truth, being
alive, was not halfway between anything. It was only to be
found by continuous excursions into either realm, and though
proportion is the final secret, to espouse it at the outset is to
ensure sterility." Proportion is the final secret, and that is why
all good marriages are what Stanley Cavell calls remarriages,
and not lust masquerading as passion. Only those who remarry
are married.

Marriage, in short, is a bargain, like buying a house or
entering a profession. One chooses it knowing that, by that
very decision, one is abnegating other possibilities. In choosing companionship over passion, women like Beatrice Webb
and Virginia Woolf made a bargain; their marriages worked
because they did not regret their bargains, or blame their husbands for not being something else—dashing lovers, for example. But in writing biographies, or one's own life, it is both
customary and misleading to present such marriages, to one-

self or to one's readers, as sad compromises, the best of a bad bargain, or scarcely to speak of them at all. Virginia Woolf mentioned that she, who is reticent about nothing, had never spoken of her life with Leonard. But we know that she said of him that when he entered a room, she had no idea what he was going to say, a remarkable definition of a good marriage. Such marriages are not bad bargains, but the best of a good bargain, and we must learn the language to understand and describe them, particularly in writing the lives of accomplished women.

I have spoken of reinventing marriage, of marriages achieving their rebirth in the middle age of the partners. This phenomenon has been called the "comedy of remarriage" by Stanley Cavell, whose *Pursuits of Happiness*, a film book, is also perhaps the best marriage manual ever published. One must, however, translate his formulation from the language of Hollywood, in which he has developed it, into the language of middle age: less glamour, less supple youth, less fantasyland. Cavell writes specifically of Hollywood movies of the 1930s and 1940s in which couples—one partner is often the dazzling Cary Grant—learn to value each other, to educate themselves in equality, to remarry. Cavell recognizes that the actresses in these movies, often the dazzling Katharine Hepburn, are what made them possible. If read not as an account of the beautiful people in hilarious situations, but as a deeply philosophical discussion of marriage, his book contains what are almost aphorisms of marital achievement. For example: "it is an essential feature of [the comedy of remarriage], as I conceive it, to leave ambiguous the question whether the man or woman is the active or the passive partner, whether indeed active and passive are apt characterizations of the difference between male and female, or whether indeed we know satisfactorily how to think about the difference between male and female" (82); and

"[The romance of remarriage] poses a structure in which we are permanently in doubt who the hero is, that is, whether it is the male or the female who is the active partner, which of them is in quest, who is following whom" (122).

Above all, despite the sexual attractiveness of the actors in the movies he discusses, Cavell knows that sexuality is not the ultimate secret of these marriages: "in God's intention a meet and happy conversation is the chiefest and noblest end of marriage. . . . Here is a reason that these relationships strike us as having the quality of friendship, a further factor in their exhilaration for us." He is wise enough, moreover, to emphasize "the mystery of marriage by finding that neither law nor sexuality (nor, by implication, progeny) is sufficient to ensure true marriage and suggesting that what provides legitimacy is the mutual willingness for remarriage, for a sort of continuous reaffirmation. . . ." "Remarriage, hence marriage, is, whatever else it is, an intellectual undertaking" (87, 88, 142, 257).

Cavell's earliest and wisest conclusion is that "only those can genuinely marry who are already married." That first, thunderous, compelling attraction must not lead to marriage because it cannot lead to remarriage; it is therefore not marriage at all, but passion, the relationship of lovers. "It is as though you know you are married when you come to see that you cannot divorce, that is, when you find that your lives simply will not disentangle. If your love is lucky, the knowledge will be greeted with laughter" (127). But it may instead be greeted with a certain amount of bickering, which is less attractive, admittedly, between two middle-aged people than between Cary Grant or Spencer Tracy and Katharine Hepburn. (Note that when Tracy and Hepburn made movies in their later years, they ceased bickering: too unattractive altogether.) But, Cavell remarks, "there may be a bickering that is itself a mark, not of bliss exactly, but of caring. As if a willingness for marriage entails a certain willingness for bickering" (86).

In short, Cavell teaches us that the happiest marriages are not always the best behaved, and that paying attention to each other in public at least indicates that a couple is involved in the relationship, as opposed to ignoring it graciously or absolutely. He concludes with an original image of the marriage bed not, as it has come to be on television and in the movies, as the setting for the spectator sport of sex, but rather "to stand for everything in marriage that is invisible to outsiders, which is essentially everything, or everything essential" (195).

Biographers have looked at marriage, and particularly at the marriages of the eminent women who are their subjects, from the outside, using only the indications of happy marriage that romance and the patriarchy have taught us. Rather, we must look, with Cavell's guidance, at that marriage in middle age that is remarriage; we must look for its conversations, for its qualities of friendship, above all, for its equality and the equality of the man's and woman's quests. The sign of a good marriage is that everything is debatable and challenged; nothing is turned into law or policy. The rules, if any, are known only to the two players, who seek no public trophies.

Five

*Affection . . . means the state of
influencing, acting upon, moving, and impressing,
and of being influenced, acted upon, moved, and
impressed by other women. Virginia Woolf
expressed this . . . when she said, "Only women
stir my imagination." She might have added, "Only
women stir me to action and power."*

—JANICE G. RAYMOND

THE WOMAN who writes herself a life beyond convention, or the woman whose biographer perceives her
as living beyond conventional expectations, has usually early recognized in herself a special gift without
name or definition. Its most characteristic indication is the
dissatisfaction it causes her to feel with appropriate gender
assignments. Willa Cather is a particularly clear example. As
Sharon O'Brien, in her biography of Willa Cather, describes
Cather's double bind: "either she could write as a woman, in
which case she created a limited art, or she could write as a
man, in which case she created an inauthentic art" (174). From
her earliest years, Cather identified the powerful with the masculine; she knew, moreover, that it was power she wanted: to
be a doctor, to dissect, to know, to speak with authority and
assertion. She despised weak men and womanly women. At
college she became William Cather in her attempt to "construct an alternative, autonomous, and powerful self," and "to

avoid becoming a platitude, a conventionally assigned identity" (99). We can scarcely imagine the courage this act required, or the pain she was willing to endure in an attempt to overcome what appeared to be her gender barrier to ambition; she wished to find the world "not fixed, but fluid" (100). Could one, in altering dress, the most prominent sign of gender, alter gender expectations?

Louisa May Alcott, like Cather, felt torn between her girl's body, the constrained female life to which it condemned her, and the freedom of male experience and possibility. She wrote to a friend: "I was born with a boys [sic] nature & always had more sympathy for & interest in them than in girls, & have fought my fight with a boys spirit under my 'bib & tucker' & a boys wrath when I got floored" (Stern, xviii).

Although the most evident mark of this gift is the sense of being a boy imprisoned in a girl's body, other female children endure, even delight in, the "feminine" aspects of their girlhood and nonetheless experience a sense of vocation, a calling, for which the expectations of their sex offer no obvious route. Examples are Edith Wharton, who wrote, without living it, Lily Bart's life, and George Eliot, who understood but did not endure the life of Dorothea Brooke. Margaret Fuller, however, like many women who as girls were possessed by unusual gifts and desires without object, regarded her young womanhood with despair: "I feel within myself great power, and generosity, and tenderness; but it seemed to me as if they were all unrecognized, and as if it was impossible that they should be used in life. I was only one-and-twenty; the past was worthless, the future hopeless, yet I could not remember ever voluntarily to have done a wrong thing, and my aspiration seemed very high" (quoted in Blanchard, 86).

The future of such gifted girls—and by *gifted* I mean not only talented but with a sense of great possibilities, great de-

sires beyond the apparent possibility of fulfillment—would seem
doubly dubious because of the lack of girl companions with
like desires. If we look at the lives of Cather, Fuller, Alcott, we
discover that it was with boys that they felt most comfortable.
The terrible dearth of girls who, like themselves, would will-
ingly sacrifice girlish charms and success for a definable ambition was profoundly felt. We have now learned, thanks to recent
historians of the female past, that not all accomplished women
were, in their heyday, as bereft of women friends as we had
thought them to be. Thomas Lash, in his book on Helen Keller
and Annie Sullivan, calls their friendship "exceptional," de-
claring there has been "nothing like it in history" (quoted in
Raymond, 174). The work of Blanche Wiesen Cook and others
has revealed the supporting group of friends behind many outstanding women in the past whose public lives could hardly
have endured without such support. We have learned to guess
how often in the past, their stories only now emerging, women
in the public sphere have loved other women, and drawn from
that love what men draw not from the companionship of other
men but from the friendship and support of women. We begin
to surmise that if we look beyond the public face of those few
notable women in the past, we may find an untold story of
friendship between women, sustaining but secret. However,
friendship between girls who aspired to more than the conventional female destiny, or who were not satisfied with the heady
reward of adolescent male attention, has been rare, at least
until the last third of this century. Certainly it went largely
unrecorded by the likes of Cather, Alcott, and Fuller.

Indeed, friendship between women has seldom been re-
counted. Women have been seen to support one another in
the crises of their lives, particularly in those family crises so
central to a woman's experience of marriage, birth, death, illness, isolation. From the love of women for one another as they

work and live side by side, however, recorders of civilization have, until the last decade, averted their eyes. (Nor is such evidence even now apparent: Letty Cottin Pogrebin quotes Margaret Thatcher as saying that without her women friends she could not have survived [279], but certainly none of these women friends have surfaced in Thatcher's political life; it is hard not to wonder whether she may be referring to her hairdresser.) If one sets out to survey the annals of friendship (as annals go, a rather short collection), one ends by reading—in Plato, Aristotle, Epicurus, Plutarch, Erasmus, Montaigne, Johnson, Rousseau, Emerson, Thoreau, et al.—of male friendships. If the friendships of women are considered at all, and that is rare enough, they intrude into the male account the way a token woman is reluctantly included in a male community.

Vera Brittain's *Testament of Friendship* is an ideal, rare counterexample: Brittain and Winifred Holtby met after World War I, as students at Somerville College, Oxford. Their friendship ended in 1937 with the death from kidney disease of Holtby. Only death could halt the friendship and its constant and continuous dialogue; neither marriage, nor distance, nor illness could have done so. When Brittain published *Testament of Friendship* in 1940, she adopted the title in keeping with her earlier, famous *Testament of Youth*, which recounts Brittain's experience in the war, the loss of her fiancé, her brother, and her male friends, and her meeting with Winifred Holtby. The title *Testament of Friendship* is an apt one: a testament serves as evidence of something. *Testament of War* would have been nearer the proper title for Brittain's *Testament of Youth*; *Testament of Friendship* exactly describes the later volume. The friendship of Vera Brittain and Winifred Holtby was an exemplary love.

When Vera Brittain in her prologue remarks that the friendships of women "have usually been not merely unsung, but mocked, belittled and falsely interpreted," she exempts from this the devotion of Ruth and Naomi in the Book of Ruth. yet friendship between a daughter and a mother-in-law is, after all, allowable if unusual within the conventional patriarchal structure. Its story, like the other familiar stories of female devotion, echoes little beyond the demands of marriage and property.

If one asks what marks all those male friendships that have been acclaimed "from the days of Homer," the answer is clear: reverberation upon the public sphere. Male friendships were not entirely, or even primarily, private; they resonated in the realms of power. Friendships for men, however intense—and the intensity, or lack of intensity, in male friendships, which are so often based on having only one activity or undertaking in common, is another matter—affect the world of event. Male friends do not always face each other: they stand side by side, facing the world. On the other hand, whatever beauty we may find in recorded affection between women, we must call their affectionate relationships, without scorn, societies of consolation. Women nourished men as they went forth to a world of activity, and consoled one another as they waited, passively and with fear, for what life might force them to endure. Where women have, rarely, gone forth to battle, it has been at the side of men. But for Brittain and Holtby, friendship meant, as it had long meant for men, the enabling bond that not only supported risk and danger but also comprehended the details of a public life and the complexities of the pain found there.

The story of Vera Brittain and Winifred Holtby is not that untold story, as Brittain knew, but it is close in many ways: "Neither of us had ever known any pleasure quite equal to the joy of coming home at the end of the day after a series of separate varied experiences, and each recounting these incidents to the other over late biscuits and tea. . . . Those years with Winifred taught me that the type of friendship which reaches its apotheosis in the story of David and Jonathan is not a monopoly of the masculine sex" (117). Jonathan had failed to kill David because they were friends, and was therefore later killed in a battle led by David. What David said at Jonathan's death is remembered, though its implications are perhaps insufficiently studied: "I am distressed for thee, my brother Jonathan: very pleasant hast thou been unto me: thy love to me was wonderful, passing the love of women." To evoke his love, attempting to describe it, David turns to another love, that of women. Similarly, Montaigne, whose essay on friendship is pivotal in any study of the subject—and it is well to remember that he, too, like David and Vera Brittain, was writing of a dead friend—ponders on what the ideal of friendship might be:

To tell the truth, the ordinary capacity of women is inadequate for that communion and fellowship which is the nurse of this sacred bond; nor does their soul seem firm enough to endure the strain of so tight and durable a knot. And, indeed, but for that, if such a relationship, free and voluntary, could be built up, in which not only the souls have this complete enjoyment, but the bodies would also share in the alliance, so that the entire man would be engaged, it is certain that the resulting friendship would be fuller and more complete. But this sex [women] in no instance has yet succeeded in attaining it, and by the common agreement of the ancient schools is excluded from it.

It has been widely assumed that women are mentioned by David as a way of saying that his love for Jonathan was a physical love, as his love for a woman would be assumed to have been. Who can assert that true friendship does not include the possibility of physical love, as the friendship of the old must include the possibility of death? By such signs do we know ourselves to be human. But beyond this, David, like Montaigne after him, realized that it is women who have long understood and embodied the essential qualities for friendship: intimacy, admission of vulnerability, the openness of the loving gesture.

Intimacy has been beyond most men, certainly beyond those men whose profound effect, usually unfortunate, has been registered in the public sphere. They have bonded with men, known sexuality with women, but been incapable of what a modern psychologist has called "a highly loving, sexually free, and emotionally intimate relationship. There are probably two reasons for this. First, in the Judeo-Christian tradition, manliness has been raised to an ideal perceived as warriorlike, free of the "softer" virtues of nurturance and gentle affection. Men, who have defined themselves as *not* women, *not* their mothers, have relegated the talents of intimacy to the female sex.

The second reason is that, given wives by the culture, men had nurturers licensed for use on the premises. They could return from the buffets of a hard world to someone who would soothe, feed, and comfort them, give them gentle reassurance, and do their laundry. (Claudia Koonz, in her study of women under Hitler, reveals this pattern as the Nazi ideal.) Men have guessed, therefore, that true friendship in some way resembled ideal marriage, though neither friendship nor marriage has attained the ideal: friendship has too much resembled for men the camaraderie of battle, for women the consolations of passivity; marriage has owed too much to romance, too little to friendship. Sexuality, too narrowly confined in marriage, has been too rigidly forbidden in friendship; both marriage and friendship have suffered from the separation of sexuality and the more general energy of love and life itself. We have not dared to say "I love my friend."

Though both Holtby and Brittain were later aware of Freud's work, and admired it, it is unlikely that either had read his "The Relation of the Poet to Day-Dreaming." Had they done so, they would have recognized his clear assertion that women daydream erotic scripts, men ambitious ones. Freud saw men as able to combine the erotic and the ambitious—there may be a woman in the dream for whom the tasks are undertaken— but for women, the ambitious is not considered as an alternative. Certainly all fiction, to say nothing of the fictive scripts that control the lives of women, set the erotic and the ambitious against each other for women. Perhaps because of all the male deaths in their generation, certainly because the war had revolutionized their priorities, Brittain and Holtby cherished and encouraged in each other ambitious dreams. Like the men in Freud's essay, they dreamed their ambitious dreams not in isolation from the erotic but possibly (should they marry) including it. If these inclusions seemed unlikely, since the men they knew and loved were either dead or damaged, nonetheless the possibility for marriage remained—to become a fact for Vera, a deathbed event for Winifred.

The remarkable friendship, beginning in 1920 and ending with Winifred's death in 1937, is preserved for us not only in *Testament of Friendship* but in the letters they wrote to each other. "Without work I am nothing," Winifred wrote in letters again and again. Because she and Vera could work together, and both felt the importance of work above all else, their friendship developed in their mutual defense, in each other's behalf, of time of their own. After Vera's marriage, Winifred helped her to struggle "against the tradition that domesticity must be the first concern of wife and mother."

Those who cherish women's friendship are fortunate in having not only *Testament of Youth* and *Testament of Friendship*, written five years after Holtby's death, but also two collections of letters, one of letters from Winifred to a friend in the women's Army Corps, the other of letters between Holtby and Brittain. This second volume, privately published in 1960 in an edition of five hundred copies and sold by subscription, is virtually unobtainable today. Winifred and Vera were together much, but whenever they were apart—and, in addition to travels, both women, being true daughters of their time, were frequently called home for services no parent today would think of demanding of a child—they wrote to each other.

In her introduction to the volume of letters between herself and Holtby, Brittain repeats a theme that would recur in many of her books on women in England: the struggle that Winifred had in finding time for her novel when she was constantly summoned home as a "heaven-sent convenience upon whom 'duty' laid the combined functions of nurse, companion, secretary and maid of all work. . . . She would try to write amid a pandemonium of interruptions . . . standing by in crises, offering consolation in illnesses, carrying minor domestic burdens of every description, and even running round the neighborhood to visit sick relatives while already conducting her own fight with death to finish *South Riding*," her important, successful, posthumous novel.

Through the hard grind toward publication and the constant stream, at first, of rejected manuscripts and bad reviews, Holtby and Brittain sustained each other. They wrote each other what sound like love letters to a world attuned to affection only between courting men and women: "I find you in all small and lovely things [Winifred writes to Vera], in the little fishes like flames in the green water, in the furred and stupid softness of bumble-bees fat as laughter, in all the chiming radiance of warmth and light and scent in the summer garden. I love you for all small and silly things."

But, sustaining as their friendship was, both women had a wide circle of friends; love begets love. They were not enclosed in an isolated relationship, a *folie à deux*, as some marriage become. The women friends of Winifred and Vera were themselves interesting and vital, proponents of feminism, activists in many causes, professionally committed. There were Viscontess Rhondda, legally her father's heir, a major figure in the publishing and political world of the time; Phyllis Bentley and Rose Macaulay, novelists; Ellen Wilkinson, a Labour MP, parliamentary private secretary, and writer of detective novels, among much else; Theodora Bosanquet, for a time secretary to Henry James (he dictated the late novels to her) and, later, secretary to the International Federation of University Women, literary editor of *Time and Tide,* and author of a book on Paul Valéry; Rebecca West; and others. Somerville College, in the years when Brittain and Holtby were undergraduates, had produced other writers: Dorothy Sayers, Margaret Kennedy, Hilda Reid—all part of what Brittain called, in *Testament of Youth,* "a universal tide then flowing so strongly toward feminism," a pronouncement that must affect feminists today with a certain wry despair for, like all tides, this one recedes with regularity.

The friendship of Vera Brittain and Winifred Holtby is as a public record, unique. It arose from the bond of two young women who wished to make their mark on the world, and to change that world in the process. No connection with a man checked, at that time, either of their destinies, nor, in the years ahead, did marriage end it. It is not surprising, therefore, that the pattern for their new friendship at Oxford, where they met, and their plans for the years ahead should have been, even unconsciously, a male pattern. They looked forward, as young men did, to leaving the university for London, work, and "life." Winifred wrote to Vera of her delight in reading just such a fictional account: "If you call yourself Rodney and me Peter it might almost be a glorified replica of some of our midnight conversations." There was no fiction for young women that seemed written to their needs.

Women's friendships are more common today, more read-

ily perceived than in the time of Brittain and Holtby. yet is is
eerie how applicable to today's world is much of what Holtby
wrote in her book *Women and a Changing Civilization.* Because so many women have yet to change their vision of what
their lives might be outside of service to males, the book sounds
almost unbearably contemporary. Holtby mentions also the
refusal of many women who lead public lives to identify themselves as feminists or to recognize their debt to other women.
In her conclusion, she writes:

I think that the real object behind our demand is not to reduce all
men and women to the same dull pattern. It is rather to release their
richness of variety. We still are greatly ignorant of our own natures.
We do not know how much of what we usually describe as "feminine
characteristics" are really "masculine," and how much "masculinity"
is common to both sexes. Our hazards are often wildly off the mark.
We do not even know—though we theorise and penalise with fero-
cious confidence—whether the "normal" sexual relationship is homo-
or bi- or hetero-sexual. We are content to make vast generalizations
which quite often fit the facts enough to be tolerable, but which—
also quite often—inflict indescribable because indefinable suffering
on those individuals who cannot without pain conform to our rough-
and-ready attempt to make all men [and women] good and happy.
[192]

All writers of women's lives, whether biographers or the
women themselves, all girls with a gift that appears to have
been vainly endowed, ought to ponder Holtby's views on
friendship and sexuality, and above all should heed her admo-
nition to walk "more delicately" where others are concerned.
Misfits are often our most gifted children and, for girls, those
most likely to require a different story by which to write their
lives.

Perhaps because Winifred loved so freely and so widely, it
did not occur to her to dream of a man "of her own." Certainly
she did not think of marriage as others thought of it: she saw a

conventional woman's life as a price not worth paying to indulge a passion for young men, or for the social assurance marriage offered. She knew the trap that caught young women was to see themselves as "sex objects," as we would say today, with "sex-success," as she called it. And though Winifred loved children, and cared for Vera's children and her own nieces for long periods of time, she did not delude herself that all women need to be with their children all the time. In Holtby's novel *The Land of Green Ginger* Joanna says: "It's awfully dangerous to make the best of a bad bargain. . . . I think I can do the best for the children by doing the best for myself. . . . The children depend on me to protect them and be wise for them. How can I be wise for them if I wasn't wise for myself? How can I help them to be more of a person than I am?" Joanna's husband is shocked that she is occasionally happy away from her children. He "cherished a thought common to many men that mothers possessed a standard of values unknown to husbands and spinsters which made the presence of their children essential to their happiness, even if it involved continual supervision."

When Brittain wrote of her friendship with Holtby, she felt she had to protect herself from accusations of lesbianism. To deny those "feminine individualists [who] believe they flatter men by fostering the fiction of women's jealous inability to love and respect one another" was easy enough. But she felt impelled also to answer those "other skeptics [who] are roused by any record of affection between women to suspicions habitual among the over-sophisticated. 'Too, *too* Chelsea!' Winifred would comment amicably in after-years when some zealous friend related the newest legend current about us in the neighborhood."

Listening to Holtby when she tells us to walk "more delicately" today must mean that love between women will extend, in what Adrienne Rich understands as an unbroken spectrum or continuum, from passionate bodily love to friend-ships between women married or living with men. Rich has testified, and all who shared her experience of early feminism can concur, that those first heady feminist discussions were erotic, and that eroticism, or energy, continues between any friends who share a passion for their work and for a body of political ideas. The sign of female friendship is not whether friends are homosexual or heterosexual, lovers or not, but whether they share the wonderful energy of work in the public sphere. These, some of them hidden, are the friends whom biographers of women must seek out.

Six

[Marilyn Monroe] was a female impersonator; we are all trained to be female impersonators.

—GLORIA STEINEM

WE MUST RECOGNIZE what the past suggests: women are well beyond youth when they begin, often unconsciously, to create another story. Not even then do they recognize it as another story. Usually they believe that the obvious reasons for what they are doing are the only ones; only in hindsight, or through a biographer's imaginative eyes, can the concealed story be surmised. I have decided, in order to illustrate the way such a story might be uncovered, to use myself as an example, analyzing the reasons why I adopted and for years kept wholly secret the pseudonym of Amanda Cross, under which, beginning in 1964, I published detective stories. Not until I had been asked repeatedly to account publicly for my decision to write detective novels under a pseudonym did I realize that the explanation I had always offered, and believed, was perhaps insufficient.

I have the impression—and I want to emphasize that it is no more than an impression—that, despite a few famous male exceptions, women write under an assumed name far more often than do men, and have done so since the early nineteenth century. Women write under pseudonyms for profound reasons that require scrupulous examination. As Gilbert and Gubar put it, "the [woman's] pseudonym began to function more prominently as a name of power, the mark of a private christening into a second self, a rebirth into linguistic primacy" (1987, 241).

Certainly I was not without coldly practical reasons when I decided to write detective novels as Amanda Cross. There was no question in my mind then, nor is there any now, that had those responsible for my promotion to tenure in the English department of the university where I teach known of the novels, they would have counted them heavily against me; I would probably have been rejected. As it happens, the professor who came up for tenure before me had written several novels—serious ones, not items of "popular culture"—and was turned down, as he supposed then, for being a novelist. I don't intend to analyze the motives behind this harsh response to English professors' forays into fiction, but harsh it is. So the practical reasons for writing under a pseudonym were clear. One had one's "real" identity, and if one chose to indulge in frivolities, however skillful, one did it under another name than that reserved for proper scholarship.

I no longer think that this was the whole explanation. I think now that there are layers within layers of significance to a woman's decision to write under a pseudonym, but the most important reason for her doing so is that the woman author is, consciously or not, creating an alter ego as she writes, another possibility of female destiny. So full of anxiety were women, before the current women's movement, when imagining alternate destinies that they wished to hide their authorial identity from prying eyes.

Charlotte Brontë, after writing to her publisher that she was "neither man nor woman," went on to say, "I come before you as an author only. It is the sole standard by which you have a right to judge me—the sole ground on which I accept your judgment." She felt, correctly no doubt, that certain scenes she had created that were considered "unfeminine" had been judged so only because she was a woman; a man would have been able to "get away with it." She wished to bring *Villette* out under what Margot Peters calls "the sheltering shadow of an incognito" (Peters, 256, 352). She had, in fact, an over- whelming desire for anonymity. And, indeed, even her best friends secretly, or not so secretly, found her novels "coarse" and unbecoming in their presentation of passion. When Mat- thew Arnold disliked *Villette* because it was so full of hunger, rebellion, rage, he was at the same time identifying its strengths, but these were unbearably presumptuous in a woman writer.

George Sand, too, chose a name other than her own, but, as we have seen, before the pseudonym came male imperson- ation, the freedom of moving like a boy. George Eliot, too, as we know, sought the safety of anonymity.

But what has all this to do with an assistant professor of English in 1964 who was hardly as restricted as those three literary giants? What does a woman setting out in the early 1960s to write a detective story have to do with the problems of women in the nineteenth century, before women had any legal identity or, indeed, any rights at all? How could someone worried about promotion in a profession, enjoying all the free- doms of action by then won for women, if not quite all the liberties of dress and movement the next decade would bring, compare herself to these women so constrained, so much the prisoners of powerful convention, so lacking a tradition of fe- male accomplishment?

I believe that women have long searched, and continue to search, for an identity "other" than their own. Caught in the conventions of their sex, they have sought an escape from gender. A woman author who was not content to expound the titillations of romance, or to live out Freud's family romance, had two means of escape. One was to hide her identity as an author within the shelter of anonymity, the safety of secrecy, to write while protecting the quotidian self leading her appropriate life. The other way was to create in her writings women characters, and sometimes male characters, who might openly enact the dangerous adventures of a woman's life, unconstrained by female propriety. Some, like Charlotte Brontë, did both. George Eliot, whose "significant other," George Henry Lewes, protected her from all assaults from public, publisher, or reviewer, did not re-create new female destinies, but examined with genius and wisdom the life of her times. Willa Cather lived a private life meticulously protected from scrutiny, and, in the words of Louise Bogan, when she was awarded Princeton's first honorary degree to a woman, Cather "well knew that she had accomplished, in the last decade or so, a miracle which would cause any university now extant to forget and forgive her sex" (Schroeter, 126). We know, however, that she dressed as a boy when in college, and was able so successfully to ghostwrite S. S. McClure's autobiography, with its account of male adventures, that not even his family suspected that he had not written it himself. She could neither fit, within the expectations for her sex, into a life that allowed the enactment of her dreams, nor discover in the public sphere a place where she could be wholly herself.

We return from this account of great names to the life of a woman in her late thirties in the year 1963. Why did she determine to write a detective novel? It certainly was not because time was hanging heavy on her hands: she had three children under the age of eight, a large dog, newly acquired, a husband who had gone back for his Ph.D. in economics, and a full-time job. Her motives were both clear and clouded. She "knew" then what her "single" motive was: she had run out of English detective novels, having read them all many times. She felt an enormous need to enter the world of fiction that the English detective-novel writers were no longer providing, or were unable to provide in sufficient numbers. Why not try to write one?

Many people have had the same thought; few enough have acted on it, for the very good reason that writing a detective novel is a lot of work, much easier to conceive than to carry through, to abandon than to complete. Only recently have I asked myself whether the urge to write them instead of reading them is, after all, a sufficient explanation, given the circumstances.

I believe now that I must have wanted, with extraordinary fervor, to create a space for myself. This was, physically, almost impossible. The cost of renting an apartment in New York City was certainly insignificant then compared to now, but for us the need for each child to have a room took precedence over my needs. I used to notice, visiting in the suburbs where so many of my contemporaries lived in those days (and from which our holdout was considered almost as eccentric as my working), that there would be a den, and a finished basement, and a laundry, and, in fact, a room for everyone but the wife / mother, who, it was assumed, had the whole house. Anne Sexton has written a very good poem about this point, which shocked many people at the time:

Housewife

Some women marry houses.
It's another kind of skin; it has a heart,
a mouth, a liver and bowel movements.
The walls are permanent and pink.
See how she sits on her knees all day,
faithfully washing herself down.

> Men enter by force, drawn back like Jonah
> into their fleshy mothers.
> A woman *is* her mother.
> That's the main thing.

If there was no space for a woman in the suburban dream house, how unlikely that there would be space in a small city apartment. So I sought, I now guess, psychic space.

But I also sought another identity, another role. I sought to create an individual whose destiny offered more possibility than I could comfortably imagine for myself. Charlotte Brontë, that genius, in creating Jane Eyre, was not more hungry or rebellious than I. Our talents are not comparable, but our impulses are. Writing even the most minor of novels, formula fiction as it is called, nonetheless teaches one a great deal about the ways of genius. (It has often occurred to me that all teachers of literature ought to have written and published a work of fiction in order to understand something fundamental about what they teach, but that is another matter.)

Many women writers used a male protagonist in their first novels: George Eliot, Charlotte Brontë, Willa Cather, May Sarton, to name a few; and among the famous women who wrote detective stories in what have come to be called the golden twenties, all featured male detectives. Some, later, created women sleuths to act with their male detectives, or instead of them—Christie's Miss Marple, Tey's Miss Pym, Sayers's Harriet Vane; indeed, a number of male detective writers also had temporary female sleuths—and the logical thing for me to have done, looking back, would have been to create a male detective. I do remember trying, very briefly, to do so, and abandoning the attempt with great haste. Here again we have a good surface reason: I simply didn't know enough about how men thought, as opposed to spoke, and I had read enough modern novels written by women but with male protagonists—Nadine Gordimer had recently written one—to know that male sexuality, to go no further, was a problem. And one did not create detectives, even in the dreary 1950s and early 1960s, wholly without sexual thoughts or experience. (Women writers in the nineteenth century had certain minor advantages.) But there was more to it than that. In our post-Freudian days—and mine was a generation that bowed down before Freud and paid constant homage—abandoning one's womanhood fictionally meant exposing oneself to terrible accusations and suspicions, far too risky for one working as hard as I was to maintain a proper wife, mother, role-playing mask. These days, when, I am glad to say, there are many women mystery writers creating sexually active women detectives, both lesbian and hetero, it is hard to think oneself back to that situation, but it was very real indeed.

I created a fantasy. Without children, unmarried, unconstrained by the opinions of others, rich and beautiful, the newly created Kate Fansler now appears to me a figure out of never-never land. That she seems less a fantasy figure these days—when she is mainly criticized for drinking and smoking too much, and for having married—says more about the changing mores, and my talents as prophet, than about my intentions at the time. I wanted to give her everything and see what she could do with it. Of course, she set out on a quest (the male plot), she became a knight (the male role), she rescued a (male) princess. Later I found Denise Levertov's lines:

> In childhood dream-play I was always
> the knight or squire, not
> the lady:
> quester, petitioner, win or lose, not
> she who was sought.

(That Kate had the help of a man is neither here nor there. We all need help. She was dependent not on any male individual but on the New York police force and the D.A.'s office, without which action was impossible.) Kate was gutsy. She also held a few opinions I now consider retrograde (such as her faith in Freud's conviction that the complaints of sexual abuse on the part of his women patients were all fantasy), but she has changed with time, she's learned, and that's all one can ask of anybody.

The question I am most often asked is how and why I chose the name "Amanda Cross." This was, or seemed at the time, a matter of no significance. My husband and I had once been stranded in a deserted part of Nova Scotia; while we awaited rescue, we contemplated a road sign reading "MacCharles Cross." My husband, attempting cheer, remarked that if either of us ever wanted a pseudonym, that would be a good one. I remembered that moment in 1963 when I finished my first detective novel, but was told that my book had obviously been written by a woman and that I should use a woman's first name. I chose "Amanda," under the (as it turned out, entirely mistaken) impression that no one since Noel Coward's early plays had had that name. In recent years, I have heard many other explanations of my choice of pseudonym: that I stole Agatha Christie's initials; that the word *cross* carries many meanings of conflict, tension, and choice, which I wanted; that the phrase *a-man-da-cross* is not without significance, and so on. I accept all of them, even the one claiming it was after Katharine Hepburn's role of Amanda in *Adam's Rib*. I didn't see that movie until a few years ago, on television. Certainly if I had, the name would have appealed to me for that reason. A word or name must bear, I agree with Coleridge, all the meanings that connotations attach to it.

I had a very good reason for secrecy, but as I now perceive, the secrecy itself was wonderfully attractive. Secrecy is power. True, one gives up recognition and publicity and fame, should any be coming one's way, but for me that was not difficult. I do not care for publicity and, because I have a regular paying job, I can afford, as a writer of detective novels, to avoid it. I think that secrecy gave me a sense of control over my destiny that nothing else in my life, in those pre-tenure, pre-women's-movement days, afforded.

(I might mention, in passing, that the secret was easily kept, because I told no one other than my husband, my agent, and my publisher. Doris Lessing, in her recent stunt of publishing novels under a pseudonym, the motives for which I shall abjure examining, found that her secret was easily kept because she did not tell any friends or acquaintances; so my instincts were proved right. But there was one awful moment. My first novel was nominated for the Edgar, awarded annually by the Mystery Writers of America for the best first novel. As E. B. White has said, it is a very satisfactory thing to win a prize before a large group of people. But winning would have blown my cover, and I prayed to lose: I was absolutely unambivalent. As it turned out, the prize was won by the first of the Rabbi novels, which was a vast relief to me.)

Meanwhile, creating Kate Fansler and her quests, I was re-creating myself. Women come to writing, I believe, simultaneously with self-creation. Sand went to Paris and dressed as a boy. Colette was locked in a room by her husband to become his ghostwriter: that was what her self demanded to take the terrible risk of writing. Even when the writing self was strengthened, only after great trouble could she leave her husband and find her own name, a single name, peculiarly marked by both feminine and—because it was her father's name—patriarchal significance.

Let me add that for female writers this act of self-creation comes later in life than for such a one as Keats. George Eliot was thirty-eight at the time her first fiction was published. So was Willa Cather. Virginia Woolf was in her thirties. This is by no means a universal rule with women writers, but it is frequent enough to be worth noticing. Acting to confront society's expectations for oneself requires either the mad daring of youth, or the colder determination of middle age. Men tend to move on a fairly predictable path to achievement; women transform themselves only after an awakening. And that awakening is identifiable only in hindsight.

There were aspects of my double life that were fun. Before the Amanda Cross secret was out, I found myself corresponding under both identities and, in one instance, writing different letters to the same person under both names. James Sandoe, well-known professor of drama and critic of mystery stories, decided on different occasions to write to Amanda Cross about her novels and to Carolyn Heilbrun about androgyny and her essay on Dorothy Sayers. Eventually I admitted to him the identity of his two correspondents.

We are only just beginning, I think, to understand the way autobiography works in fiction, and fiction in autobiography. Consider, for example, the question of mothers in novels. Florence Nightingale, writing of her despair at a life without occupation or purpose, commented on how young women pass their time by reading novels in which "the heroine has generally no family ties (almost invariably no mother), or, if she has, they do not interfere with her entire independence." The heroines of most novels by women have either no mothers, or mothers who are ineffectual and unsatisfactory. Think of George Eliot; think of Jane Austen; think of the Brontës. As a rule, the women in these novels are very lonely; they have no women friends, though they sometimes have a sister who is a friend.

What was the function of mothers toward daughters before the current women's movement, before, let us say, 1970? Whatever the drawbacks, whatever the frustrations or satisfactions of the mother's life, her mission was to prepare the daughter to take her place in the patriarchal succession, that is, to marry, to bear children (preferably sons), and to encourage her husband to succeed in the world. But for many women, mothers and daughters alike, there moved in their imaginations dreams of some other life: of personal accomplishment, of the understanding and control of hard facts and complex problems, of a place in a community where women were in sufficient numbers to render the accomplished woman neither lonely nor an anomaly. Above all, the dream of taking control of one's life without the intrusion of a mother's patriarchal wishes for her daughter, without the danger of injuring the much loved and pitied mother.

When, safely hidden behind anonymity, I invented Kate Fansler, I gave her parents, already dead, whom she could freely dislike, and create herself against, although they had been good enough to leave her with a comfortable income. (So Samuel Butler, writing *The Way of All Flesh*, recommended that all children be deserted at birth, wrapped in a generous portion of pound notes.) Carolyn Heilbrun had, in fact, great affection for her parents, great admiration for her father and a sense of affectionate protectiveness toward her mother. But they were conservative people; they could not understand her wish to remake the world and discover the possibility of different destinies for women within it. Amanda Cross could write, in the popular, unimportant form of detective fiction, the destiny she hoped for women, if not exactly, any longer, for herself: the alternate life she wished to inscribe upon the female imagination.

It is of the very first importance to realize, however, that Carolyn Heilbrun in 1963 was not dissatisfied with her life. She was not, like Florence Nightingale, or Charlotte Brontë isolated at Haworth, dreaming of some event to rescue her. She believed then, as now, that her life was a full and satisfactory one, with every promise of becoming more so. When she sought psychic space, it was not from personal frustration but rather from a wish, characteristic of almost every woman writer who did not write erotic romances, for more space, less interruption, more possibility of adventure and the companionship of wiser women through these adventures, greater risk and a more fearless affronting of destiny than seemed possible in the 1950s and early 1960s.

How much of this wish to transform female destiny was conscious? None of it. I suspect that if I had been told then that my depriving Kate Fansler of parents indicated any ambivalence on my part toward my parents, I would have disputed that conclusion with vigor. All the conscious reasons for writing were good ones; they operated, they were sufficient to explain my actions. Yet the real reasons permitted me, as other women have found ways to permit themselves, to write my own life on a level far below consciousness, making it possible for me to experience what I would not have had the courage to undertake in full awareness. I think Virginia Woolf, for example, early realized, deeply if unconsciously, that the narratives provided for women were insufficient for her needs. Her life and her works, the equal to any by her contemporaries, have been until recently less studied academically because we quite literally did not have the language, the theory, or the perceptions with which to analyze them. All her novels struggle against narrative and the old perceptions of the world. She felt in herself a powerful need for a love we have come to call maternal, a love that few men are able to offer (outside of romance) and that women have been carefully trained not to seek in other women. Virginia Woolf found a nurturing man to live with, and she found women to love her. She needed to be loved, and she knew it. Most of us women, I think, transform our need to be loved into a need to love, expecting, therefore, of men and of children, more than they, caught in their own lives, can give us. But Woolf, whether from need or genius, or both, knew that when Chloe and Olivia worked side by side in a laboratory, when women had a room of their own and money of their own (which is power), the old story of woman's destiny, the old marriage plot, would give way to another story for women, a quest plot.

So women like Carolyn Heilbrun in 1963, and writers of an earlier time, seeking some place outside Freud's family romance, wrote out, under other names or in hidden stories, their revolutionary hopes.

Women have long been nameless. They have not been persons. Handed by a father to another man, the husband, they have been objects of circulation, exchanging one name for another. That is why the story of Persephone and Demeter is the story of all women who marry: why death and marriage, as Nancy Miller pointed out in *The Heroine's Text*, were the only two possible ends for women in novels, and were, frequently, the same end. For the young woman died as a subject, ceased as an entity. For this reason, then, women who began to write another story often wrote it under another name. They were inventing something so daring that they could not risk, in their own person, the frightful consequences.

Let me return, after these grand statements about famous women and female destiny, to my two names adopted so cavalierly twenty-five years ago. Something happened to both Carolyn and Amanda: the women's movement. Carolyn began writing in a more personal, for her more courageous, manner, recognizing that women could not speak to other women as men had always spoken, as though from on high. She wrote of herself, she told her own story, she risked exposure: going public was still a chancy thing for a woman, but not as chancy as it had been, because there were more women doing it.

And Amanda became more openly courageous too: she wrote of feminist matters, and let her heroine continue to smoke and drink, despite frequent protests from readers. I think too much drinking is a fearful affliction, and I don't smoke, but Kate Fansler has stuck to her martinis and cigarettes as a sort of camouflage for her more revolutionary opinions and actions. For some reason, I was reluctant to reform her, to tell her how to behave. My hope, of course, is that younger women will imitate her, not in smoking and drinking, not necessarily in marrying or declining to have children, but rather in daring to use her security in order to be brave on behalf of other women, and to discover new stories for women. She is, oddly, no longer a fantasy figure but an aging woman who battles despair and, one hopes with a degree of wit and humor, finds in the constant analysis of our ancient patriarchal ways, and in sheer effrontery, a reason to endure.

Kate Fansler has aged less rapidly than do mortals, but inexorably. And it is she, rather than the persona "Amanda Cross," who has come to be a presence in my life. When I have not written about her for a while, she makes her presence known. Biographers have sometimes written, as have fiction writers, of the palpable existence of their subjects. I remember reading once that Simenon, when he had ignored Maigret for many months, would find him waiting around corners, silently confronting his creator, demanding incarnation, or at least attention. So it has been with Kate. And when I recently promised not to begin a new detective novel until I had finished another, different kind of book, she would not let me be. So for the first time I wrote short stories about her, told by her niece Leighton Fansler as a kind of Watson. Though I have often thought in the past that I would write no more detective novels, I now think that I shall probably be forced to write them as long as Kate is there to nudge me.

Kate Fansler has taught me many things. About marriage, first of all. I could see no reason for her to marry: there was no question of children. But, insisting upon marrying, she taught me that a relationship has a momentum, it must change and develop, and will tend to move toward the point of greatest commitment. I don't wholly understand this, but I accept it, learning that the commitment of marriage, which I had taken for granted, has its unique force. But it is about aging that she has taught me most. She is still attractive, but no longer beautiful, and unconcerned with her looks. Her clothes she regards as a costume one dons for the role one will play in the public sphere. Her beauty was the only attribute I regreted bestowing, and age has tempered that, although, unlike her creator, she is still a fantasy figure in being eternally slim. But most important, she has become braver as she has aged, less interested in the opinions of those she does not cherish, and has come to realize that she has little to lose, little any longer to risk, that age above all, both for those with children and those without them, is the time when there is very little "they" can do for you, very little reason to fear, or hide, or not attempt brave and important things. Lear said, "I will do such things, what they are yet I know not, but they shall be the terrors of the earth." He said this in impotent rage in his old age, but Kate Fansler has taught me to say it in the bravery and power of age.

Seven

---

*Time and trouble will tame an advanced
young woman, but an advanced old woman is
uncontrollable by any earthly force.*

—DOROTHY L. SAYERS

F OR WOMEN who have awakened to new possibilities
in middle age, or who were born into the current
women's movement and have escaped the usual
rhythms of the once traditional female existence,
the last third of life is likely to require new attitudes and new
courage. Virginia Woolf is an example of a woman who found a
new and remarkable kind of courage when she was fifty. This
is, I believe, an achievement uniquely female. At fifty Virginia
Woolf began work on *The Years* and *Three Guineas*, both of
which to this day affront the sensibilities of almost all her male
critics. To allow oneself at fifty the expression of one's feminism
is an experience for which there is no male counterpart, at least
for white men in the Western world. If a man is to break into
revolt against the system he has, perhaps for his parents' sake,
pretended to honor, he will do so at a much younger age. The
pattern of men's lives suggests that at fifty they are likelier to
reveal their egoism than their hidden ideals or revolutionary
hopes. I mention this to emphasize what has been so little
understood by Woolf's biographers, editors, and, apparently,

even by Leonard Woolf himself: the nature of what happened to her in her fifties.

In Woolf's decision to express her sense of society's deprivation of women, she had two major obstacles to fear. The first was the ridicule, misery, and anxiety the patriarchy holds in store for those who express their anger about the enforced destiny of women. That not even Leonard could understand this condemns not Leonard, but the profound influence of the system that has served men so well. Even today, after two decades of feminism, young women shy away from an emphatic statement of anger at the patriarchy. Perhaps only women who have played the patriarchal game and won a self despite it can find the courage to consider facing the pain that the outright expression of feminism inevitably entails. It is worth noting that writers and critics who would have modulated their language in other contexts felt free then (and now) to indulge in tirades against feminist attitudes. Woolf knew what she had to fear, but at fifty she thought she had found the courage to bear it.

The second obstacle was within herself: her own sense of the importance to literature of separating art and propaganda (to put it in its harshest terms, which she never failed to do); she saw art and discursiveness as opposed, and the presentation of "fact" inimical to art. Her sense of art, which had with the force of a religious principle forbidden "propaganda," was the hardest obstacle to overcome. Profoundly felt principles are often the bedrock on which the structure of our sanity rests. It was this second obstacle, of course, that Leonard spoke of when he said she was writing against the grain. Quentin Bell, Woolf's biographer, saw *The Years* as "a step back, or at least a step in another direction. It could easily be a wrong direction" (vol. 2, 195). For Bell and others, anger would be retrogressive.

The tone of *Three Guineas* is angry; Woolf, like all women, had to fight a deep fear of anger in herself. (For many years I was made uncomfortable by *Three Guineas*, preferring the "nicer" *A Room of One's Own*, where Woolf never presses against the bounds of properly charming female behavior; I say this to my shame.) It's well worth noting, however, that while Woolf struggled long and desperately with *The Years*, she found, in her ability in *Three Guineas* to say the unacceptable, an extraordinary release. She, who had worried so about reviews, did not even bother to read Queenie Leavis's virulent attack all the way through. From first to last, *Three Guineas* was a romp, possible, perhaps, only after fifty. All her life Woolf had written against such anger, had, indeed, castigated Charlotte Brontë for this very fault. To discover in one's fifties the courage to go against this conviction is as triumphant as it is rare.

It is perhaps only in old age, certainly past fifty, that women can stop being female impersonators, can grasp the opportunity to reverse their most cherished principles of "femininity." Here again they differ from men, who need discover new courage, perhaps, but need not profoundly change their lives, need not dedicate them to something new, only perhaps more intensely to their old ambitions. Henry James, as he approached the age he and others could call elderly, wrote in his notebook:

The upshot of all such reflections is that I have only to let myself *go!* So I have said to myself all my life—so I said to myself in the far-off days of my fermenting and passionate youth. Yet I have never fully done it. The sense of it—of the need of it—rolls over me at times with commanding force: it seems the formula of my salvation, of what remains to me of a future. I am in full possession of accumulated resources—I have only to use them, to insist, to persist, to do something more—to do much more—than I *have* done. The way to do it— to affirm one's self *sur la fin*—is to strike as many notes, deep, full and rapid, as one can. All life is—at my age, with all one's artistic soul the record of it—in one's pocket, as it were. Go on, my boy, and

strike hard; have a rich and long St. Martin's summer. Try everything, do everything, render everything—be an artist, be distinguished to the last. [106]

Two friends from James's youth, Henry Adams and Oliver
Wendell Holmes, were, like James, to flower late: Adams did
not write *Mont-Saint-Michel and Chartres* until he was sixty-
five and his *Education of Henry Adams* until he was seventy.
Holmes was appointed to the Supreme Court when he was
sixty-one. Men have seemed able to achieve a life beyond the
usual active span. Samuel Butler tells us that Fontenelle, the
eighteenth-century French writer and Secretary of the Royal
Academy of Science, on being asked at the age of ninety what
had been the happiest time of his life, said he did not know
that he had ever been much happier than he then was, but that
perhaps his best years had been those between the ages of fifty-
five and seventy-five.

Can we find no similar examples among women? May Sarton's fame is greater now that she is seventy-five than it has
ever been. Doris Grumbach became a novelist very late. Stevie
Smith wrote: "I am becoming quite famous in my old age, isn't
it funny how things come round?" (313). Colette, as we have
already noted, came into her own only at the age of fifty. Käthe
Kollwitz, when old, wrote in her diary that she found familial
ties growing slacker: "for the last third of life there remains
only work. It alone is always stimulating, rejuvenating, exciting and satisfying" (Kearns 125).

Fiction has recently dared to delineate a kind of old-age
freedom for women. Toni Morrison writes of Pilate in *The Song
of Solomon:*

When she realized what her situation in the world was and would
probably always be she threw away every assumption she had learned
and began at zero. First off, she cut her hair. That was one thing she
didn't want to think about anymore. Then she tackled the problem of

trying to decide how she wanted to live and what was valuable to her.
When am I happy and when am I sad and what is the difference?
What do I need to know to stay alive? What is true in the world? Her
mind traveled crooked streets and aimless goat paths, arriving sometimes at profundity, other times at the revelations of a three-year-
old. Throughout this fresh, if common, pursuit of knowledge, one
conviction crowned her efforts: since death held no terrors for her
(she spoke often to the dead), she knew there was nothing to fear.
[149]

Yet, for the rare Toni Morrison portrait, we have many
more like this from a novel by Anne Tyler—portraits of women
clinging to a life and conditions they have in fact outgrown,
instead of launching off into another world. Here is an aged
woman from Tyler's *The Clock Winder:*

She had once been very pretty. She still was, but now that her
children were grown there was something brave about the pretti-
ness. She had started having to work for it. She had to fight the urge
to spend her days in comfortable shoes and forget her chinstrap and
let herself go. . . . Her face was a series of pouches tenuously joined
by transparent skin, reminding her of the tissue-covered frames of
model airplanes that her sons used to make. Her close-set blue eyes
were divided by minute cracks. Her mouth had bunched in upon
itself so that she permanently wore the sulky look she had once had
as a child. All she had left was color—pink, white, blond, most of it
false. Weekly she went to the hairdresser and returned newly gilded,
with her scalp feeling tight as if it were drawing away from her face.
She dressed up for everything, even breakfast. She owned no slacks.
Her thin, sharp legs were always in ultra-sheer stockings, and her
closet was full of those spike-heeled shoes that made her arches ache.

"Women," an Isak Dinesen character says, in contrast, "when
they are old enough to have done with the business of being
women, and can let loose their strength, must be the most
powerful creatures in the world."
Yet few women think of old age and power as compatible

ideas for them. As Dorothy Richardson observed, the shock "is a threshold shock. A door is closing behind us and we turn sorrowfully to watch it close and do not discover, until we are wrenched away, the one opening ahead." Most women never discover it, because we cannot believe it is there. Too few of us even ask questions of our old age. Too few of us ask, as Rich does: "Dear Adrienne:/I'm calling you up tonight/as I might call up a friend as I might call up a ghost/to ask what you intend to do/with the rest of your life." Rich can ask this question because she knows "not all of them will love you whichever way you choose" (1986b 88, 48).

In the end, the changed life for women will be marked, I feel certain, by laughter. It is the unfailing key to a new kind of life. In films, novels, plays, stories, it is the laughter of women together that is the revealing sign, the spontaneous recognition of insight and love and freedom. Recently we have begun to notice the perfunctoriness of the endings of Jane Austen's novels. She has had to tie up the ends, to finish her heroines off in the only acceptable way. In the end there is never laughter, but at best contentment, at worst a kind of vague disquiet. Elizabeth, in *Pride and Prejudice,* the most romantic of the novels, says of Darcy at the end that he is not yet ready to be laughed at, or with, and there is no woman with whom to share laughter. Austen probably laughed a good deal with her sister and her nieces, but laughter did not mark the high point of any of her adventures or the adventures of her heroines. Women laugh together only in freedom, in the recognition of independence and female bonding.

And with laughter comes the end of fantasy and daydreaming. Bertha Pappenheim, a patient of Freud's known as Anna O, indulged in what Dianne Hunter calls systematic daydreaming; Pappenheim called it her "private theater." As Hunter puts it, "people left to embroidery are bound to embroider fantasies" (94). It was Pappenheim's transition from daydreaming to speech that marked her cure. Women like Florence Nightingale and Beatrice Webb who found their way to a meaningful life identified daydreaming as a sign of their meaningless lives and the only consolation for them. The acceptance of a new challenge in middle or old age marks the end of fantasy, and the substitution, as with Käthe Kollwitz and others, of work. It marks also the end of the dream of closure.

We women have lived too much with closure: "If he notices me, if I marry him, if I get into college, if I get this work accepted, if I get that job"—there always seems to loom the possibility of something being over, settled, sweeping clear the way for contentment. This is the delusion of a passive life. When the hope for closure is abandoned, when there is an end to fantasy, adventure for women will begin. Endings—the kind Austen tacked onto her novels—are for romance or for daydreams, but not for life. One hands in the long-worked-on manuscript only to find that another struggle begins. One gets a job to find new worries previously unimagined. One achieves fame only to discover its profound price. Somehow men have known this, but women rarely, if at all. But with the coming of age can come such knowledge. Sometimes, as with Woolf, or Anne Sexton, or others we have all known, it can lead to the trough of despair, and to the sense of life as without value, or at least of oneself as without the necessary courage or desire. But most often, particularly with the support of other women, the coming of age portends all the freedoms men have always known and women never—mostly the freedom from fulfilling the needs of others and from being a female impersonator.

I once titled an Amanda Cross detective novel *Death in a Tenured Position*, and it occurs to me now that as we age many of us who are privileged—not only academics in tenured positions, of course, but more broadly those with some assured place and pattern in their lives, with some financial security— are in danger of choosing to stay right where we are, to undertake each day's routine, and to listen to our arteries hardening. I do not believe that death should be allowed to find us seated comfortably in our tenured positions. Virginia Woolf described this condition in *Mrs. Dalloway:* "Time flaps on the mast. There we stop; there we stand. Rigid, the skeleton of habit alone upholds the human frame. Where there is nothing" (55). Instead, we should make use of our security, our seniority, to take risks, to make noise, to be courageous, to become unpopular.

Biographers often find little overtly triumphant in the late years of a subject's life, once she has moved beyond the categories our available narratives have provided for women. Neither rocking on a porch, nor automatically offering her services as cook and housekeeper and child watcher, nor awaiting another chapter in the heterosexual plot, the old woman must be glimpsed through all her disguises which seem to preclude her right to be called woman. She may well for the first time be woman herself.

Works Cited

Abel, Elizabeth. "(E)merging Identities: The Dynamics of Female Friendship in Contemporary Fiction by Women." *Signs* 6, no. 3 (Spring 1983): 413–35.

Ackroyd, Peter. *T.S. Eliot.* New York: Simon & Schuster, 1984.

Ascher, Carol. *Simone de Beauvoir: A Life of Freedom.* Boston: Beacon Press, 1981.

Ascher, Carol, Louise DeSalvo, and Sara Ruddick, eds. *Between Women: Biographers, Novelists, Critics, Teachers and Artists Write About Their Work on Women.*

Auden, W. H. *Forewards & Afterwards.* New York: Vintage Books, 1974.

Auerbach, Nina. *Communities of Women.* Cambridge: Harvard University Press, 1976.

———. *Woman and the Demon.* Cambridge: Harvard University Press, 1982.

Bayley, John. *The Characters of Love.* New York: Basic Books, 1960.

Bell, Quentin. *Virginia Woolf: Volume One: Virginia Stephen; Volume Two: Mrs. Woolf.* London: Hogarth Press, 1972.

Blanchard, Paula. *Margaret Fuller: From Transcendentalism to Revolution.* New York: Delacorte Press, 1978.

Brabazon, James. *Dorothy L. Sayers.* New York: Scribner 1981.

Brittain, Vera. *Testament of Friendship.* London: Macmillan, 1940. Rpt. London: Virago, 1980.

Bromwich, David. "The Uses of Biography." *The Yale Review* 73, no. 2 (1984): 161–76.

Brownstein, Rachel M. *Becoming a Heroine: Reading About Women in Novels.* New York: Viking, 1982.

Cameron, Deborah. *Feminism and Linguistic Theory.* London: Macmillan, 1985.

Carter, Angela. *The Sadeian Woman.* New York: Pantheon, 1978.

Cavell, Stanley. *Pursuits of Happiness: The Hollywood Comedy of Remarriage.* Cambridge: Harvard University Press, 1981.

Clifford, James L., ed. *Biography as an Art.* New York: Oxford University Press, 1962.

Conway, Jill. "Convention versus Self-Revelation: Five Types of Autobiography by Women of the Progressive Era." Project on Women and Social Change, Smith College, Northampton, MA, June 13, 1983.

Cook, Blanche Wiesen. " 'Women Alone Stir My Imagination:' Lesbianism and the Cultural Tradition." *Signs* 4, no. 4 (Summer 1979): 718–39.

Cooper, Jane. *Maps and Windows.* New York: Collier Books, 1974.

Crawford, Mary, and Roger Chaffin. "The Reader's Construction of Meaning: Cognitive Research on Gender and Comprehension." *Gender and Reading: Essays on Readers, Texts, and Contexts,* ed. Elizabeth A. Flynn and Patrocinio P. Schweickart. Baltimore: Johns Hopkins University Press, 1986.

Daiches, David. *Virginia Woolf.* Norfolk, CT: New Directions, 1942.

De Lauretis, Teresa. *Alice Doesn't: Feminism, Semiotics, Cinema.* Bloomington: Indiana University Press, 1984.

Dinesen, Isak. "The Monkey." In *Seven Gothic Tales.* New York: Vintage Books, 1972, pp. 109–63.

Eakin, Paul John. *Fictions in Autobiography: Studies in the Art of Self-Invention.* Princeton: Princeton University Press, 1985.

Edwards, Lee R. *Psyche as Hero: Female Heroism and Fictional Form.* Middletown, CT: Wesleyan University Press, 1984.

Erikson, Erik H. *Identity: Youth and Crisis.* New York: Norton, 1968.

Fallaci, Oriana. "Conversation with Oriana Fallaci." In Jonathan Cott, *Forever Young.* New York: Random House, 1977.

Fetterley, Judith. "Reading about Reading: 'A Jury of her Peers,' 'The Murders in the Rue Morgue,' and 'The Yellow Wallpaper.' " *Gender and Reading: Essays on Readers, Texts, and Contexts,* ed. Elizabeth A. Flynn and Patrocinio P. Schweickart. Baltimore: Johns Hopkins University Press, 1986.

Finkel, Anita. "Dancing Together: The Art of Partnering at New York City Ballet." New York City Ballet Program, 85th New York Season / Nov. 18, 1986–Feb. 22, 1987 / New York State Theater. Programs of January 8, 1987, and February 5, 1987.

Frye, Northrup. *The Secular Scripture: A Study of the Structure of Romance.* Cambridge, MA: Harvard University Press, 1976.

Gardiner, Judith Kegan. "Mind Mother: Psychoanalysis and Feminism." In *Making a Difference: Feminist Literary Criticism,* ed. Gayle Greene and Coppelia Kahn. New York: Methuen, 1985, pp. 113–45.

Gilbert, Sandra, and Susan Gubar. *The Madwoman in the Attic.* New Haven: Yale University Press, 1979.

———. *No Man's Land.* Vol. 1. New Haven: Yale University Press, 1987.

Graves, Robert. *Goodbye to All That.* Garden City, NY: Doubleday Anchor Books, 1957.

Gunn, Janet Varner. *Autobiography: Toward a Poetics of Experience.* Philadelphia: University of Pennsylvania Press, 1982.

Holtby, Winifred. *Women and a Changing Civilization*. New York: Longmans, Green, 1935. Rpt. Chicago: Cassandra Edition, Academy Press, 1978.

Homans, Margaret. " 'Her Very Own Howl': The Ambiguities of Representation in Recent Fiction." *Signs* 9 (1983): 186–205.

Hone, Ralph E. *Dorothy L. Sayers: A Literary Biography*. Kent, Ohio: Kent State University Press, 1979.

Hull, Gloria T., Patricia Bell Scott, and Barbara Smith, eds. *All the Women Are White, All the Blacks Are Men, But Some of Us Are Brave*. New York: Feminist Press, 1982.

Hunter, Dianne. "Hysteria, Psychoanalysis, and Feminism: The Case of Anna O." In *The (M)other Tongue: Essays in Feminist Psychoanalytic Interpretation*. ed. Shirley Nelson Garner, Claire Kahane, Madelon Sprengnether. Ithaca: Cornell University Press, 1985.

Irigaray, Luce. "When Our Lips Speak Together," trans. Carolyn Burke. *Signs* 6, no. 1 (Autumn 1980): 69–79.

Jacobus, Mary. "The Difference of View." In *Women Writing and Writing About Women*, ed. Mary Jacobus. New York: Barnes and Nobel, 1979, pp. 10–21.

James, Henry. *The Notebooks of Henry James*, ed. F. O. Matthiessen and Kenneth B. Murdock. New York: Oxford University Press, 1947.

Jehlen, Myra. "Archimedes and the Paradox of Feminist Criticism." *Signs* 6, no. 4 (1984): 575–601.

Johnson, Diane. *The True History of the First Mrs. Meredith and Other Lesser Lives*. New York: Knopf, 1972.

Kakutani, Michiko. "A Life in Pictures." *New York Times.* June 28, 1986.

Kaplan, Cora. "Pandora's Box: Subjectivity, Class and Sexuality in Socialist Feminist Criticism." *Making a Difference: Feminist Literary Criticism*, ed. Gayle Greene and Coppelia Kahn. New York: Methuen, 1985, pp. 146–76.

Kearns, Martha. *Käthe Kollwitz: Woman and Artist*. Old Westbury, NY: Feminist Press, 1976.

Kizer, Carolyn. *Mermaids in the Basement*. Port Townsend, WA: Copper Canyon Press, 1984.

Koonz, Claudia. *Mothers in the Fatherland: Women, The Family, and Nazi Politics*. New York: St. Martin's Press, 1987.

Kreyling, Michael. "Words into Criticism: Eudora Welty's Essays and Reviews." In *Eudora Welty: Critical Essays*, ed. Peggy Whitman Prenshaw. Jackson: University Press of Mississippi, 1979, pp. 411–22.

Krull, Marianne. *Freud and His Father*, trans. Arnold J. Pomerans. New York: Norton, 1986.

Kumin, Maxine. *The Privilege*. New York: Harper & Row, 1965, pp. 79–82.

———. *To Make a Prairie*. Ann Arbor: University of Michigan Press, 1979a.

———. *The Retrieval System*. New York: Penguin, 1979b.

Levertov, Denise. *Relearning the Alphabet*. New York: New Directions, 1970.

Lewis, C. S. *The Four Loves*. London: Fontana Books, 1960.

Lorde, Audre. *The Cancer Journals*. Argyle, NY: Spinsters, Ink, 1980.

————. *Chosen Poems: Old and New*. New York: Norton, 1982.

McCabe, James. "A Woman Who Writes." In *Anne Sexton: The Artist and Her Critics*, ed. J. D. McClatchy. Bloomington: Indiana University Press, 1978, pp. 216–43.

Macdonald, Barbara, and Cynthia Rich. *Look Me in the Eye: Old Women, Aging and Ageism*. San Francisco: Spinsters, Ink, 1984.

Marks, Elaine. "Breaking the Bread: Gestures Toward Other Structures, Other Discourses." *Bulletin of the MMLA* 13, no. 1 (Spring, 1980): 55.

Martin, Wendy. *An American Triptych: Anne Bradstreet, Emily Dickinson, Adrienne Rich*. Chapel Hill: University of North Carolina Press, 1984.

Mason, Mary G. "The Other Voice: Autobiographies of Women Writers." In *Autobiography: Essays Theoretical and Critical*, ed. James Olney. Princeton: Princeton University Press, 1980, pp. 207–35.

Meese, Elizabeth A. *Crossing the Double-Cross: The Practice of Feminist Criticism*. Chapel Hill: University of North Carolina Press, 1986.

Middlebrook, Diane. "Becoming Anne Sexton." *Denver Quarterly* 18, no. 4 (Winter 1984): 23–34.

Miller, Nancy K. *Subject to Change: Reading Feminist Writing*. New York: Columbia University Press, 1988.

Moers, Ellen. "Introduction." *George Sand: In Her Own Words*, ed. Joseph Barry. Garden City, NY: Anchor Books, 1979, pp. ix–xxii.

Moglen, Helene. *Charlotte Brontë: The Self Conceived*. New York: Norton, 1976.

Morrison, Toni. Interview with Claudia Tate. *Black Women Writers at Work*, ed. Claudia Tate. New York: Continuum, 1983, pp. 117–31.

Nestor, Pauline. *Female Friendships and Communities: Charlotte Brontë, George Eliot, Elizabeth Gaskell*. New York: Oxford University Press, 1985.

Nicolson, Nigel, ed. "Introduction." *The Letters of Virginia Wolf: Volume II: 1912–22*. New York: Harcourt Brace Jovanovich, 1976, pp. xiii–xxiv.

Nightingale, Florence. *Cassandra*. New York: Feminist Press, 1979.

Nord, Deborah Epstein. *The Apprenticeship of Beatrice Webb*. Amherst: University of Massachusetts Press, 1985.

O'Brien, Sharon. *Willa Cather: The Emerging Voice*. New York: Oxford University Press, 1987.

Okely, Judith. *Simone de Beauvoir*. New York: Virago / Pantheon, 1986.

Owen, Ursula, ed. *Fathers: Reflections by Daughters*. New York: Pantheon Books, 1985.

Peters, Margot. *Unquiet Soul*. Garden City, NY: Doubleday, 1975.

Pogrebin, Letty Cottin. *Among Friends*. New York: McGraw-Hill, 1987.

Raymond, Janice G. *A Passion for Friends: Toward a Philosophy of Female Affection*. Boston: Beacon Press, 1986.

Rich, Adrienne. *Of Women Born: Motherhood as Experience and Institution.* New York: Norton, 1976.

———. *On Lies, Secrets, and Silence.* New York: Norton, 1979.

———. *The Fact of a Doorframe: Poems Selected and New 1950–1984.* New York: Norton, 1984.

———. *Blood, Bread, and Poetry: Selected Prose 1979–1985.* New York: Norton, 1986a.

———. *Your Native Land, Your Life: Poems.* New York: Norton, 1986b.

Rose, Phyllis. *Writing on Women: Essays in a Renaissance.* Middletown, CT: Wesleyan University Press, 1985.

Rubin, Gayle. "The Traffic in Women: Notes on the Political Economy of Sex." In *Toward an Anthropology of Women,* ed. Rayna R. Reiter. New York: Monthly Review Press, 1975, pp. 157–210.

Rule, Jane. *Lesbian Images.* Garden City, NY: Doubleday, 1975.

Sand, George. *My Life,* trans. and adapted by Dan Hofstadter. New York: Harper Colophon, 1979.

Sarde, Michele. *Colette,* trans. Richard Miller. New York: Morrow, 1980.

Sarton, May. *Plant Dreaming Deep.* New York: Norton, 1968.

———. *Journal of a Solitude.* New York: Norton, 1973.

Sayers, Dorothy L. "Are Women Human?" *Unpopular Opinions.* London: Victor Gallancz, 1946, pp. 106–15.

Schroeter, James, ed. *Willa Cather and Her Critics.* Ithaca: Cornell University Press, 1967.

Sexton, Anne. *A Self-Portrait in Letters,* ed. Linda Gray Sexton and Lois Ames. Boston: Houghton Mifflin, 1977a.

———. "Interview." *Writers at Work: The Paris Review Interviews,* 4th ser., ed. George Plimpton. New York: Penguin Books, 1977b, pp. 403–24.

———. *The Complete Poems.* Boston: Houghton Mifflin, 1981.

Showalter, Elaine. "Feminist Criticism in the Wilderness." In *Writing and Sexual Difference,* ed. Elizabeth Abel. Chicago: University of Chicago Press, 1982, pp. 9–36.

———. *The Female Malady: Women, Madness, and English Culture, 1830–1980.* New York: Pantheon Books, 1985.

Silver, Brenda. "Anger, Authority, and Tones of Voice: The Case of *Three Guineas*" (unpublished ms.).

Smith, Stevie. *Me Again: Uncollected Writings of Stevie Smith,* ed. Jack Barbera and William McBrien. London: Virago, 1981.

Spacks, Patricia. *Imagining a Self.* Cambridge: Harvard University Press, 1976.

———. "Selves in Hiding." In *Women's Autobiography,* ed. Estelle C. Jelinek. Bloomington: Indiana University Press, 1980, pp. 112–32.

Spalding, Frances. *Vanessa Bell.* New York: Ticknor & Fields, 1983.

Spurling, Hilary. "I. Compton-Burnett: Not One of Those Modern People." *Twentieth Century Literature* 25, no. 2 (1979): 153–64.

Stern, J. K. "The Social and the Moral Problem." In Norton Critical Edition of Tolstoy's *Anna Karenina*, ed. George Gibian. New York: Norton, 1970, pp. 856–65.

Stern, Madeleine B. "Introduction." *The Selected Letters of Louisa May Alcott*, ed. Joel Myerson and Daniel Shealy. Assoc. Ed. Madeleine B. Stern. Boston: Little, Brown, 1987.

Stimpson, Catharine R. "Gertrice / Altrude: Stein, Toklas, and the Paradox of the Happy Marriage." In *Mothering the Mind: Twelve Studies of Writers and Their Silent Partners*, ed. Ruth Perry and Martine Watson Brownley. New York: Holmes & Meier, 1984, pp. 122–39.

Stubbs, Jean. "Cousin Lewis." In *Women and Fiction*, ed. Susan Cahill. New York: New American Library, 1975, pp. 268–87.

Thomson, Patricia. *George Sand and the Victorians*. New York: Columbia University Press, 1976.

Todd, Janet. *Women's Friendship in Literature*. New York: Columbia University Press, 1980.

Tolstoy, Leo. "Letters, Diaries, and Newspapers," in Norton Critical Edition of *Anna Karenina*, ed. George Gibian. New York: Norton, 1970, p. 751.

Walker, Alice. *In Search of Our Mothers' Gardens*. New York: Harcourt Brace Jovanovich, 1983.

Weigle, Marta. *Spiders and Spinsters: Women and Mythology*. Albuquerque: University of New Mexico Press, 1982.

Welty, Eudora. "A Note on Jane Austen." *Shenandoah* 20, no. 3 (1969): 3–7.

———. Interview. *Writers at Work: The Paris Review Interviews*, 4th ser., ed. George Plimpton. New York: Penguin Books, 1977, pp. 273–92.

———. *One Writer's Beginnings*. Cambridge: Harvard University Press, 1984.

Woolf, Virginia. *A Room of One's Own*. New York: Harcourt, Brace, 1929.

———. "George Eliot." In *Women and Writing*, ed. and with an introduction by Michele Barrett. New York: Harcourt Brace Jovanovich, 1979, pp. 150–60.

Index

Nightingale, Florence, 23, 118, 119, 130
Norton, Caroline, 15

Oates, Joyce Carol, 40
O'Brien, Sharon, 96
Odyssey (Homer), 46
old age, 126–31
O Pioneers! (Cather), 43
Owen, Ursula, 64
Ozick, Cynthia, 40

Pankhurst, Emmeline, 22
Pappenheim, Bertha, 129
Persuasion (Austen), 43
Peters, Margot, 111
Plath, Sylvia, 63, 69, 70, 71, 72, 73, 74
Plato, 99
plots, *see* narratives
Plutarch, 99
Pogrebin, Letty Cottin, 99
Poovey, Mary, 15
power, 16–18, 43–44, 96, 116
  in language, 43–44
  in old age, 126–29
pseudonyms, women's, 109–12, 116–18, 121
  see also, Cross, Amanda; Sand, George; Sayers, Dorothy L.
Pride and Prejudice (Austen), 129

Raymond, Janice G., 96
Redgrave, Vanessa, 87
Reid, Hilda, 105
Rhondda, Viscontess, 105
Rich, Adrienne, 63, 65, 66–69, 71, 72–73, 107–8, 129
  early career, 66–68
  marriage, 69
  relationship with father, 69
  "What Is Possible," 73

  see also, World War II
Roethke, Theodore, 63
romances, 38–39
  see also, narratives
Roosevelt, Eleanor, 22
Rose, Phyllis, 29–30
Rousseau, Jean Jacques, 23, 99
Rowbotham, Sheila, 65
Rubáiyát of Omar Khayyám, 19
Rubin, Gayle, 81
Ruddick, Sara, 64
Rukeyser, Muriel, 74
Rule, Jane, 79
Ruth, Book of, 100

Sand, George, 33–37, 42, 111, 117
Sandoe, James, 118
Sappho, 70
Sarton, May, 12, 74, 114, 127
Sartre, Jean Paul, 44
Saxton, Martha, 82
Sayers, Dorothy L., 48, 50–59, 82, 105, 118, 124
  and Christianity, medieval studies, 58–59
  early career, 52–53
  marriage, 53
Scarlet Letter, The (Hawthorne), 43
Schorer, Mark, 12
Sexton, Anne, 63, 64, 69, 70, 71, 72, 73, 113, 130
"Shalott, the Lady of," 20
Shaw, George Bernard, 49, 87
Sheean, Vincent, 31
Showalter, Elaine, 68
Silver, Brenda, 15
Smith, Stevie, 127
Snodgrass, W. D., 63, 64, 68
Snow, C. P., 51
Somerville College, Oxford, 99, 105

About the Author

CAROLYN G. HEILBRUN is the Avalon Foundation Professor in the Humanities at Columbia University and the author of *Toward a Recognition of Androgyny* and *Reinventing Womanhood*. She has published eight mysteries under the pseudonym of Amanda Cross.